The Lord's Priesthood Word of Wisdom Standard

A History of Obedience, Sin, and Imposition

A personal revelation and the Oath and Covenant of the
Priesthood clarify the Word of Wisdom

New Evidences for Joseph Smith Series

Volume 2

The Lord's Priesthood Word of Wisdom Standard

A History of Obedience, Sin, and Imposition

A personal revelation and the Oath and Covenant of the Priesthood clarify the Word of Wisdom

Neil David Holland

Copyright 2018
ISBN 9798554411731

Independently Published
Neil D. Holland
1419 Tamarisk Dr.
Saint George, UT 84790 U.S.A.

New Evidences for Joseph Smith Series

The New Evidences for Joseph Smith Series publishes independent research by Neil David Holland. These topics were researched as Neil sought to strengthen his testimony of the Prophet Joseph Smith and the Restoration of the Gospel of Jesus Christ.

Titles marked below with * were assigned by the Lord within Neil's stewardship over his life, health, and right to equal justice. These topics were addressed to The Church of Jesus Christ of Latter-day Saints in a *Report to President Nelson* in 2018/19 to identify and correct areas of apostasy in the Church. These apostasies are from not upholding the rights of God's children to – protect one's life (D&C 134), govern one's health (D&C 89), bring charges against a President of the High Priesthood (D&C 107), and removed in 2020, the right to half of the High Council if accused (D&C 102).

The author is grateful to see a partial restoration of his right to govern his own health as given in D&C 89 by President Nelson's correction to Word of Wisdom policy in the December 2020 General Handbook. This action confirms the apostasy from the Word of Wisdom begun under President Brigham Young. Just as President Lorenzo Snow restored the Law of Tithing, and President Kimball restored the Priesthood for all men, President Nelson has partially restored the Word of Wisdom. D&C 134, 107, and 102 yet remain.

Published Volumes in the Series:
    Vol 1: *Book of Mormon Geography – Confirming the Prophet Joseph Smith's Continental View*
    Vol 2: **The Lord's Priesthood Word of Wisdom Standard*
Forthcoming works in the Series:
    The Doctrine of Our Father: Agency, Accountability, Atonement, and Advancement
    The Millennial Kingdom of God
    * Protect the Saints and Support the Lord's Constitution
    * The Lord's Justice System
    The Nature of our Galaxy
    The Nature of Light and Matter
    The Nature of Space
    Nephi's Wooden Bow

See also YouTube: *New Evidences for Joseph Smith.*

A photographic copy of an original daguerreotype taken of
Joseph Smith Jr., in Nauvoo just before his death. It was
submitted to the Library of Congress in 1879 by his son
Joseph Smith III.
http://photographfound.com/

Table of Contents

<u>**THE WORD OF WISDOM REVELATION FOR REFERENCE:**</u>
(Emphasis on **administration** and **proscriptions**)

Doctrine and Covenants (D&C) 89:
1 A **Word of Wisdom**, for the benefit of the council of high priests, assembled in Kirtland, and the church, and also the saints in Zion—
2 To be sent greeting; **not by commandment or constraint, but by revelation and the word of wisdom, showing forth <u>the order and will of God in the temporal salvation of all saints</u> in the last days**—
3 Given for **<u>a principle with promise</u>**, adapted to the capacity of the weak and the weakest of all saints, who are or can be called saints.
4 Behold, verily, thus saith the Lord unto you: In consequence of evils and designs which do and will exist in the hearts of conspiring men in the last days, I have warned you, and forewarn you, by giving unto you this word of wisdom by revelation—
5 That inasmuch as any man drinketh **<u>wine or strong drink</u>** among you, behold it **is not good**, neither meet in the sight of your Father, **only** in assembling yourselves together **to offer up your sacraments** before him.
6 And, behold, **this should be wine, yea, pure wine of the grape of the vine, of your own make**.
7 And, again, **strong drinks are not for the belly, but for the washing of your bodies**.
8 And again, **<u>tobacco</u> is not for the body**, neither for the belly, and is not good for man, but is an herb for bruises and all sick cattle, to be used with judgment and skill.
9 And again, **<u>hot drinks</u> are not for the body** or belly.
10 And again, verily I say unto you, all wholesome herbs God hath ordained for the constitution, nature, and use of man—
11 Every herb in the season thereof, and every fruit in the season thereof; all these to be used with prudence and thanksgiving.
12 Yea, **<u>flesh also of beasts and of the fowls of the air</u>**, I, the Lord, have ordained for the use of man with thanksgiving; nevertheless they are **to be used sparingly**;
13 And it is pleasing unto me that they should not be used, **only in times of winter, or of cold, or famine.**

14 All grain is ordained for the use of man and of beasts, to be the staff of life, not only for man but for the **beasts of the field, and the fowls of heaven, and all wild animals** that run or creep on the earth;

15 And these hath God made for the use of man **only in times of famine and excess of hunger**.

16 All grain is good for the food of man; as also the fruit of the vine; that which yieldeth fruit, whether in the ground or above the ground—

17 Nevertheless, wheat for man, and corn for the ox, and oats for the horse, and rye for the fowls and for swine, and for all beasts of the field, and barley for all useful animals, and for mild drinks, as also other grain.

18 And all saints who remember to keep and do these sayings, walking in obedience to the commandments, shall receive health in their navel and marrow to their bones;

19 And shall find wisdom and great treasures of knowledge, even hidden treasures;

20 And shall run and not be weary, and shall walk and not faint.

21 And I, the Lord, give unto them a promise, that the destroying angel shall pass by them, as the children of Israel, and not slay them. Amen.

10

OVERVIEW

An honest assessment of The Church of Jesus Christ of Latter-day Saints' (the Church) administration of the Lord's Word of Wisdom, from the Prophet Joseph Smith to the present, reveals a history of obedience followed by sin and then imposition.

Personal revelation that is enlightening to the member is included, but binding Word of Wisdom standards for the Church are the stewardship of the Prophet. A discussion on how the Lord's standard used by the Prophet Joseph Smith could apply today is included.

This topic was originally assigned to me by the Lord within my personal stewardship over my health. The Lord tasked me to submit this in a *Report to President Nelson* in 2018. As this book goes to print a December 2020 change to Word of Wisdom policy suggests that this period of imposition may be coming to an end and the original understanding of the Word of Wisdom as was maintained by the Prophet Joseph Smith may yet be fully restored through President Russell M. Nelson. I do not know if my *Report to President Nelson* helped to generate this change, but a significant objection to Word of Wisdom restrictions in the Church Handbook from at least 2010 and into 2020 was presented in the 2018 Report.

Word of Wisdom History: Obedience to Sin to Imposition:

Obedience (1833-1844):

The Prophet Joseph Smith required obedience to the 1833 revelation for men to receive the Melchizedek priesthood and remain in leadership. Obedience to the Word of Wisdom was not required for baptism. High Council meetings in 1834, the trial and release of the Missouri Presidency in 1838, and the record of elders ordained in 1843 confirm this standard. In 1843 the Prophet vigorously opposed strict "abstinence" for all as "pharisaical and hypocritical."

Sin (1844-1921):

After Joseph's death, Church leaders fell into disobedience, led by the Prophet Brigham Young. He, and succeeding prophets, debated if the Word of Wisdom was a commandment, for the Lord stated it was "not by commandment or constraint, but ... show(ed) forth the order and will of God." The Church claim that the Word of Wisdom became a commandment by vote at the September 1851 Conference of the Church is not supported by the Conference minutes and subsequent records. At that conference, members (except men over 90) "covenant(ed) to leave off the use of tobacco, whisky, and all things mentioned in the Word of Wisdom." In October General Conference, 1862, the Prophet Brigham Young admitted becoming obedient in 1860. In 1877, he required those receiving recommends for the first-in-the-west St. George Temple, "must observe and keep the Word of Wisdom according to the Spirit and meaning thereof." That standard was not maintained.

Imposition (1921-Present) rather than "greeting ... revelation and ... wisdom":

In 1921, President Heber J. Grant again required obedience for a temple recommend and in 1930 for missionaries, thus partially restoring the Lord's standard used by the Prophet Joseph Smith. However, he later required obedience for investigators and all members. No revelation making the Word of Wisdom a "commandment for all" was published or claimed.

The 2010 up until December 2020 Handbook went well beyond the Lord's proscribed "wine or strong drink ... tobacco ... (and) hot drinks (defined as tea and coffee by the Prophet Joseph)." It stated, "Members should not use any substance that contains illegal drugs. Nor should members use harmful or habit-forming substances except under the care of a competent physician." There was no published or claimed revelation expanding the Lord's proscriptions. However, the Lord's proscription that the "flesh also of beasts and ... fowls ... (are) to be used sparingly ... only in times of winter, or of cold, or famine" receives little emphasis other than members being encouraged generally to live the Word of Wisdom.

President Russell M. Nelson's update to the Word of Wisdom in December 2020 removes the additional restrictions that could only be used "under the care of a competent physician", except for marijuana.

The Handbook now states:

> 38.7.13.
>
> "… Prophets have clarified that the teachings in Doctrine and Covenants 89 include <u>abstinence from</u> tobacco, strong drinks (alcohol), and hot drinks (tea and coffee).
>
> "Prophets have also taught members to <u>avoid</u> substances that are harmful, illegal, or addictive or that impair judgment.
>
> "There are other harmful substances and practices that are not specified in the Word of Wisdom or by Church leaders. Members should <u>use wisdom and prayerful judgment</u> in making choices to promote their physical, spiritual, and emotional health."

… and for marijuana:

> 38.7.9
>
> <u>"The Church opposes the use of marijuana for non-medical purposes</u>.
>
> "… The Church does not approve of vaping marijuana unless the medical provider has authorized it based on medical necessity.
>
> "The Church does not approve of smoking marijuana, including for medical purposes."

The Church still insists that "The Word of Wisdom is a commandment of God" (Handbook 38.7.13) while the only claimed revelation from the Lord states it is "not by commandment or constraint" (D&C 89: 2) and Church claims that it became a commandment in 1851 under President Brigham Young are not supported by the historic record including any claimed revelation from the Lord to President Brigham Young.

Understanding *The Lord's Priesthood Word of Wisdom Standard*:

Preparing for the Sacrament in May 2018, the Lord gave me a clear understanding of the "principle" underlying the Word of Wisdom and other principles the Lord had tasked me to study as a son of God, and to report to President Nelson. The Lord told me that Russell M. Nelson is His Prophet. This personal revelation did not violate the Prophet's stewardship – it honored mine. The Lord said to me:

> **"Anything that doth enslave the soul of man is not of God, but of him that desireth that all men might be miserable like unto himself."**

Because the Word of Wisdom allows fish and animal products such as milk and eggs, and "flesh also of beasts and … fowls … used sparingly," the Word of Wisdom is not veganism or vegetarianism.

The Lord's administrative guideline "not by commandment or constraint, but … showing forth the order and will of God" (D&C 89: 1-3), debated by prophets following Joseph Smith, is actually precise and provides a transition to obedience for any person entering the Church through baptism. I call this *The Lord's Priesthood Word of Wisdom Standard*. It appears to have been understood and practiced by the Prophet Joseph Smith, but then the Church departed from it and remains confused by the Lord's statement. It is not appropriate or necessary for us to change the Lord's words from "not by commandment" to "commandment for all."

1. The covenants of baptism include one to "keep His commandments" (Mosiah 18: 8-10). The Lord declared the Word of Wisdom to be "<u>not by commandment or constraint</u>." Therefore, it must not be required for baptism.
2. His Word of Wisdom also "(shows) forth the <u>order</u> and will of God" (D&C 89:2) which has two meanings:
    a. The natural <u>order</u>. Following the natural "<u>order</u> and will of God" provides "temporal salvation."
    b. "the holiest <u>order</u> of God" (D&C 84: 18) entered through Priesthood ordination or temple ordinances. By baptism we qualify for the Celestial Kingdom. Through the Oath and Covenant of the Priesthood and obedience to "every word [of wisdom] … from … God" (D&C 84: 43-44 [33-48]) we are exalted.

How the Word of Wisdom can be Administered under *The Lord's Priesthood Word of Wisdom Standard*:

As in Joseph Smith's day, those suffering addictions that are not sin, could be received by baptism into the Church, to be "nourished by the good word of God" (Moroni 6: 4) and the gift of the Holy Ghost, as they rely upon the Savior's atonement for recovery. Word of Wisdom obedience would apply to men and women embracing the Oath and Covenant of the Priesthood at some point following baptism.

The administration of the Word of Wisdom is the responsibility of the current prophet who has the keys necessary to receive direct revelation for the Church. While confusion at the highest levels of the Church is evident throughout this history, never-the-less this is the Lord's Church and while the facts can be embarrassing, the author has no intent to criticize Church leadership – they are accountable to the Lord, as we all are.

Until the Church explains "not by commandment or constraint, but … showing forth the order and will of God" (D&C 89:2) or provides a direct revelation from the Lord modifying the original revelation, it remains at odds with the Lord's word by making the Word of Wisdom a commandment for all members – except for meat. Until the Church addresses the Lord's meat proscription it falls short of the Lord's revealed "will." It is the author's desire that the Church grow in beauty and splendor by greater acceptance of the Lord's Word of Wisdom. It is time to restore the Lord's Word of Wisdom as it was revealed and follow it as the Prophet Joseph Smith required.

The kindness of the Lord in revealing to me a better understanding of the Word of Wisdom was done within my personal stewardship over my health. The Lord was honoring this stewardship and not violating President Nelson's. This was clearly stated in the *Report to President Nelson* in 2018. I believe that the Church will yet return to the Word of Wisdom administration practiced by the Prophet Joseph Smith. The period of sin was from not following the Joseph Smith standard. The period of imposition came from the common practice of bureaucrats to constrain others to their views – not from revelation – else why so many changes? Was the Lord uncertain of His course? How could D&C 89:2 confound men who knew how to receive knowledge from God? If the Lord had not spoken to clarify it, why add to the Lord's word and impose their own understanding?

CHAPTER ONE

THE LORD'S PRIESTHOOD WORD OF WISDOM STANDARD
(as practiced by the Prophet Joseph Smith)

The Prophet Joseph Smith, Jr.

Questions arose about whether electronic cigarettes or legal Marijuana smoking violate the Word of Wisdom standard of not using "tobacco." Other Word of Wisdom questions have been raised over the years such as the use of caffeine, kava, and betel nuts. Others question why the Lord's restriction that meat be used "sparingly" is not emphasized by the Church. Additionally, questions remain as to why the Lord declared that the Word of Wisdom was "To be sent greeting; not by commandment or constraint ...."

For the past ten years at least, when Word of Wisdom questions were posed to the First Presidency, their answer had been consistently:

1. Doctrine and Covenants, Section 89 (D&C 89)
2. "The only official interpretation of "hot drinks" ... is the statement made by early Church leaders that the term ... means tea and coffee." Handbook (Before Dec 2020) 38.7.13 [Stated by Joseph and Hyrum Smith.]
3. "Members should not use any substance that contains illegal drugs." Handbook (Before Dec 2020) 38.7.13.
4. "Nor should members use harmful or habit-forming substances except under the care of a competent physician." Handbook (Before Dec 2020) 38.7.13.
5. The 1851 vote of the Church under the Prophet Brigham Young to live the Word of Wisdom as a "commandment"
6. Members are encouraged to use wisdom

With the change to Word of Wisdom policy in the December 2020, Handbook, numbers 2, 3, and 4 will change as follows:

2. "Prophets have clarified that the teachings in Doctrine and Covenants 89 include abstinence from tobacco, strong drinks (alcohol), and hot drinks (tea and coffee)." (38.7.13)

3. "... avoid substances that are harmful, illegal, or addictive or that impair judgment." (38.7.13)

4. "The Church opposes the use of marijuana for non-medical purposes ... does not approve of vaping marijuana unless the medical provider has authorized it ... does not approve of smoking marijuana." (38.7.9)

Church records made available to historians indicate that the Lord has not spoken directly to Church leaders to add revelation beyond D&C 89. The December 2020 policy return to the D&C 89 "not(s)" and Joseph Smith statements appears to confirm this in part. A timeline of Church history with regards to the Word of Wisdom is provided in the APPENDIX. Church policy has evolved through much prayer and discussion and has been focused on having "all saints" apply its principles. From President Brigham Young to President Heber J. Grant, presidents of the Church have varied in their views on how to apply the Word of Wisdom. Church leaders were also influenced in the early 1900's by Protestant movements for the prohibition of alcohol and smoking cessation.

The Prophet Joseph Smith's decision that ordination to the Priesthood and any leadership position in the Church required Word of Wisdom obedience was not continued or emphasized following his martyrdom and was not reinstated until 1921 under President Heber J. Grant. However, within a few more years under President Grant, the Lord's word that the Word of Wisdom is "not by commandment or constraint" was changed by the Church into a commandment for "all saints," including applicants for baptism, without any direct revelation from the Lord being claimed, cited, published, and sustained by the Church. The brethren have required obedience to "the order and the will of God" for "all saints" while the Lord's word "not by commandment or constraint" remains the only published revelation on the matter and His proscriptions on meat are not emphasized by the Church. A requirement for Word of Wisdom obedience for ordination to, or Temple covenants under, the Oath and Covenant of the Priesthood (D&C 84: 33-48), as applied by the Prophet Joseph Smith, has not been understood and practiced even to the present.

The Church history of Word of Wisdom administration can be summarized as obedience, sin, and imposition. The Prophet Joseph Smith administered the Word of Wisdom by requiring those under the Oath and Covenant of the Priesthood to be obedient. Following his martyrdom, the Prophet Brigham Young led the Church into a period of sin as he and many other priesthood leaders failed to be obedient. The Prophet Heber J. Grant returned the Church to obedience (except for meat) for those under the Oath and Covenant of the Priesthood for a brief period which was followed quickly by the current imposition of the Word of Wisdom on all members and candidates for baptism. This is not put forward as a criticism, but rather an accurate report of Church history. While others may tend to play down and even avoid the facts, we are better served by understanding the truth our history reveals – else how can we as a Church repent? The Lord by revelation can redirect the living Prophet with respect to the Word of Wisdom, just as He directed Peter to extend the gospel opportunity to the gentiles, President Wilford Woodruff with respect to ending polygamy, President Lorenzo Snow to restore obedience to the Law of Tithing, and President Spencer W. Kimball to "confirm(ed) (that) … every faithful, worthy man in the Church may receive the holy priesthood … without regard for race or color (Official Declaration 2)." No such revelation has been claimed or published as the history of the Word of Wisdom clearly shows. The Church claim that the Word of Wisdom became a commandment under the Prophet Brigham Young in 1851, is not supported by Church records. The Lord's Word of Wisdom remains the only direct revelation on the subject and awaits our faithful obedience.

A. Personal Revelation Received in May 2018

In May 2018, after having studied, prayed and meditated on this topic for several weeks, I received the following personal revelation just prior to partaking the Sacrament:

> **"Anything that doth enslave the soul of man is not of God, but of him that desireth that all men might be miserable like unto himself."**

I immediately recorded this as it had come from outside myself – simply entering my mind as "pure intelligence flowing into (me)." (Teachings of the Prophet Joseph Smith, p.151)

Hearing the "voice of the Lord" as described by Enos (Enos 1: 5, 10) is a gift of the Spirit that I seem to have inherited from my father, Arthur. He first experienced God call him by name, **"Arthur"**, as a young boy and then while serving in the Royal New Zealand Air Force in World War II, **"Arthur."** These calls led him to later investigate the Church. Following his baptism, he was shaving one morning and considering whether or not he could afford to pay a full tithing. The voice of the Lord came to him, **"Arthur. If you remain faithful you will die mourned by thousands."** He served the Lord faithfully the rest of his life, serving as a Sealer in the New Zealand temple for many years before he passed on. Such experiences in hearing the voice of the Lord have been a great blessing to me and my family. The above personal revelation is one example of a few I will share.

This personal revelation is enlightening to the individual member seeking to understand the Word of Wisdom but does not change the administration of the Word of Wisdom which is given by the Lord in D&C 89: 1-3, and which falls under the stewardship of the Lord's living Prophet.

The revelation provides great insight into the "principle with promise" underlying the "revelation and the word of wisdom." It supports in part the Church General Handbook (before Dec 2020) 38.7.13 statement against "harmful or habit-forming substances." It establishes the principle upon which the Word of Wisdom proscriptions were given. "Anything that doth enslave the soul of man is not of God …." There are numerous things beyond "Tobacco", "wine or strong drink", and "hot drinks" which "enslave the soul …" through addiction, disease, or mind alteration. We have all understood this by medical deduction, but here was the word of the Lord removing any doubt for me.

As a missionary serving in the Church's Addiction Recovery Program, this enlightenment allowed me to see how Satan puts us in bondage through many means. To name only a few:

1. Tobacco (Nicotine)
2. Alcohol
3. Prescription drugs (Opioids etc.)
4. Legal and unregulated drugs of many kinds (Caffeine, Kava, Betel Nut)
5. Illegal drugs of many kinds (Heroin, Meth, etc)

6. Sexual lust and Pornography
7. Refined Sugar and carbohydrates and resulting disease
8. Excessive meat consumption and resulting disease
9. Gambling
10. Unrighteous dominion over others (Co-dependency)
11. Victimhood and Fear

Many things that "enslave the soul" often go unrecognized by the individual. Life's challenges reveal these addictions, time reveals disease. Many of these addictions, such as victimhood, fear, mild codependency, sugar, etc., are not sins. Though one's "temporal salvation" is affected, developing an extensive list of proscribed substances and practices is impractical and unnecessary.

Life reveals enslavements and allows the individual opportunity to overcome through self-discipline and the Atonement of Jesus Christ. For example:

> My challenges with fear originated in my childhood. My fear came in many forms and led to codependency, unresolved issues, self-limiting success, and debt. It took many years for me to recognize my fears and to overcome them with the Lord's help.
>
> As Branch President of the Khamis Mushayt Branch, Arabian Peninsula Stake, in 1999, I feared to follow an impression from the Spirit that would have resolved a problem – I did not follow the Spirit's direction.
> Not long after, while attending a Church Leadership Conference in Bahrain, the Lord chastised me, **"Neil, you have allowed fear to limit your faith. It is time to put fear aside and trust completely in the Lord."** I then received an instruction which I followed, and for the next year I felt like an onion, as the Lord identified and peeled away one layer of fear after another. It was only recently, while serving as a missionary in the Addiction Recovery Program that I recognized another layer of fear that was so supple that I had not noticed it, despite it being responsible for my poor financial decisions and enslavement to debt.

The word "soul" in the revelation is very accurate. The enslavement affects spirit and body – the soul (D&C 88:15). Use of the words "enslave the soul" is very instructive. Being a slave is not a sin – it is a condition that "is not of God." It is a reference to Satan, who "leadeth them by the neck with a flaxen cord, until he bindeth them with his strong cords forever (2 Ne 26:22)." Sin may have brought about the enslavement, and sins may be committed while enslaved, but the enslavement is not sin. We treat with compassion the enslaved or addicted soul, encouraging him to repent of any past sins and to not sin again – to be forgiven of his sins and to overcome his addiction through the Atonement of Jesus Christ.

Satan seeks to "enslave the soul of man" through many means. Again, we have all understood this by scriptural deduction, but here was the word of the Lord removing any doubt for me. Scriptural examples of this principle include:

> Stand fast therefore in the liberty wherewith Christ hath made us free, and be not entangled again with the yoke of bondage. (Galatians 5: 1)

> For when they speak great swelling words of vanity, they allure through the lusts of the flesh, through much wantonness, those that were clean escaped from them who live in error. While they promise them liberty, they themselves are the servants of corruption: for of whom a man is overcome, of the same is he brought in bondage. (2 Peter 2:18-19)

Many additional scriptures can be reviewed by following the "bondage" footnotes in the scriptures.

The revelation was enlightening to me as I sought to understand the Word of Wisdom, but it does not address the administration of the Word of Wisdom which is the stewardship of the Prophet of the Lord's Church. This is in keeping with the Lord's principle of revelation. My health is my stewardship and the Lord provided me revelation within my stewardship and did not violate the Prophet's.

However, as one who is under the Oath and Covenant of the Priesthood, I am now obliged to stay away from "Anything that doth enslave the soul of man" because I am to "live by every word that proceedeth forth from the mouth of God" (D&C 84: 43-44 [33-48]) – in this case to me personally.

The following observations from this personal revelation are intended only for consideration as Church leaders ponder the mind and will of God, short of a direct revelation from Him:

The revelation supports the prior-to-Dec-2020 Handbook's legal but "harmful or habit-forming substances" but does not proscribe them or require "the care of a competent physician" for permission to use.

The Lord does not change His "Word of Wisdom" into a commandment. The language of the original revelation "To be sent greeting; not by commandment or constraint ..." is not modified.

It is also true that the "will of God in the temporal salvation of all saints in the last days" is not modified. It is God's will that we obey the Word of Wisdom. "And all saints who remember to keep and do these sayings, walking in obedience to the commandments, shall receive ....":

1. "temporal salvation"
2. "health in their navel and marrow to their bones"
3. "find wisdom and great treasures of knowledge, even hidden treasures"
4. "shall run and not be weary, and shall walk and not faint."
5. "the destroying angel shall pass by ... and not slay them."

The proscriptions of D&C 89: "Tobacco", "wine or strong drink", "hot drinks", and "flesh also of beasts and of the fowls ... are to be used sparingly" are not identified as sin and remain the only proscriptions the Lord has spoken through direct revelation. However, some things that "enslave the soul of man" are sins already identified by the Lord and are used as standards for baptism, priesthood ordination, and temple recommends:

1. Taking illegal drugs of many kinds (Heroin, Meth, etc.) violate the laws of the land

2. Sexual lust and pornography involve physical and virtual
   adultery or fornication and therefore violate the Lord's law of
   chastity:
   a. 3 Ne 12:27-30 "Behold, it is written by them of old
       time, that thou shalt not commit adultery; but I say
       unto you, that whosoever looketh on a woman, to lust
       after her, hath committed adultery already in his heart
       ...."
   b. James 1:14-15 "But every man is tempted, when he
       is drawn away of his own lust, and enticed. Then
       when lust hath conceived, it bringeth forth sin: and
       sin, when it is finished, bringeth forth death."

B. Understanding the Lord's Word Of Wisdom Administrative Guidelines (D&C 89: 1-3)

Following the personal revelation, I was led to review the Lord's
Word of Wisdom administrative verses (D&C 89: 1-3). What does
the Lord mean "not by commandment or constraint" and yet
"showing forth the order and the will of God" for "all saints" with
respect to their "temporal salvation"?

I asked myself, "Is God confused in saying it is not a commandment,
and yet it is His will? No!"

And, "Should we be confused? I believe not."

And, "Have we understood what He means? Perhaps not."

Then why "not by commandment or constraint, but ... the order and
will of God"?

1. God's Natural "Order"

The Lord has said, "… it is not meet that I should command in all things; for he that is compelled in all things, the same is a slothful and not a wise servant; wherefore he receiveth no reward. Verily I say, men should … do many things of their own free will, … for the power is in them, wherein they are agents unto themselves. And inasmuch as men do good they shall in nowise lose their reward." (D&C 58: 26-28) The Lord did not therefore "(command) or (constrain)", but rather provided "wisdom … by revelation" highlighting commonly used substances of Joseph Smith's day, believed by many to be good, but contrary in their use to "the order and will of God (for our) temporal salvation." We are therefore left to choose as "agents unto ourselves" to follow "the order and will of God." We can choose to follow this "principle with promise, (which is) adapted to the capacity of the weak and the weakest of all saints."

The First Presidency and Kirtland High Council in 1834 referred to "neglecting to comply with and obey" the Word of Wisdom as a "transgression" rather than a sin. All transgression is a failure to follow the laws of God, whether declared (Ten Commandments) or in nature (smoking leads to lung cancer). All transgression, however, is not sin. One example is Adam and Eve who transgressed a commandment of God and suffered the fall. The term sin is not used because Adam and Eve were not accountable, not knowing the difference between good and evil. Likewise, young children below the age of accountability do not sin when they transgress God's laws. The Lord's declaration that the Word of Wisdom is "not by commandment or constraint" suggests that disobedience to it is not a sin against God or our fellow man and is therefore not under God's judgement other than the natural consequences He established and a higher order of life He offered.

For an accountable person, breaking a commandment is a sin of commission, for which he is judged and "constraint(s)" or punishments assigned. When we consider the Ten Commandments, they all cover sins against God or our fellow man. On the other hand, the Word of Wisdom is associated with sins against ourselves. When we transgress the natural "order" which God established, we suffer the consequences. None of us would intentionally burn our bodies. The resulting natural effect of pain and death is a natural order we avoid.

The Lord's introduction is therefore very precise. Commandments require obedience or the judgement of God. In the case of the Word of Wisdom, violating this "principle with promise" results in the natural "order" harming our "temporal salvation" – we bring it upon ourselves. Conversely, obedience brings forth "health."

However, there is an added consideration for those who enter the Oath and Covenant of the Priesthood. Those who had entered that covenant following the 1832 revelation (D&C 84), will have recognized the 1833 Word of Wisdom revelation as a commandment for them as the "will of God."

2. The "Holiest order of God"

For the Prophet Joseph Smith, and the Kirtland and Missouri High Councils in 1834, the Word of Wisdom was a "transgression" that would disqualify one from the responsibilities of leadership under the Oath and Covenant of the Priesthood. In Nauvoo, in 1840, the Prophet vigorously opposed enforcing a policy of abstinence for all Saints by calling it "pharisaical and hypocritical." For all members of the Church, the Word of Wisdom is available to follow and benefit from without the "constraint" of a "commandment." God is not a dictator. He defends the liberty and agency of His children by "commandment and constraint" to protect the rights of each child. Liberty and agency end where we violate the rights of our fellow man whether under the influence of proscribed substances or not. Other than by the natural order, God does not "constrain" us for the harm we do ourselves by not living the Word of Wisdom. Within the proper use of our agency, we are invited to come unto Christ, to be "anxiously engaged in a good cause and bring to pass much righteousness," to live the "principle" of the Word of Wisdom, to take upon us the Oath and Covenant of the Priesthood, and to enter the Temple abode of God. However, over time, like the well-intentioned Elder in Nauvoo, Church leaders have constrained the whole Church, and those seeking to enter it, by being "pharisaical and [in President Brigham Young's case] hypocritical" by calling the Word of Wisdom a commandment for all without any claimed revelation in which the Lord revokes His "greeting; (given) not by commandment or constraint." It was Satan who sought to "destroy the agency of man" in order to dictate salvation for all. The Elder in Nauvoo, Church leaders following Joseph Smith, and men today, tend to impose good behavior mistaking their action as righteousness.

When the revelation was given, investigators and new members were not "command(ed) and constrain(ed)" or judged by the Lord for not living the Word of Wisdom. It was not something to be repented of for baptism. Nevertheless, it did declare "the order and will of God" which members were wise to follow. It offered many blessings for their "temporal salvation."

The covenants made at baptism do not include one to observe a personal health code but do include a covenant to "keep His commandments" and the Lord declared the Word of Wisdom to be "<u>not by commandment or constraint</u>."

Alma details baptism's conditions and covenants (Mosiah 18: 8-10):
1. "as ye are desirous to come into the fold (Church) of God, and to be called his people,
2. and are willing to bear one another's burdens, …;
3. Yea, and are willing to mourn with those that mourn;
4. yea, and comfort those that stand in need of comfort,
5. and to stand as witnesses of God at all times and in all things, and in all places that ye may be in, even until death, that ye may be redeemed of God, and be numbered with those of the first resurrection, that ye may have eternal life— Now I say unto you, if this be the desire of your hearts, what have you against being baptized in the name of the Lord,
6. as a witness … ye have entered into a covenant with him,
7. that ye will serve him and
8. keep his commandments, that he may pour out his Spirit more abundantly upon you?

Since the Lord did not give the Word of Wisdom "by commandment or constraint" then it holds that the Word of Wisdom does not need to be repented of for baptism and a remission of sins. Once a member, the Lord brings the individual under the Word of Wisdom by commandment when they take on the Oath and Covenant of the Priesthood upon ordination for a Brother, or when a Sister enters these covenants through Temple ordinances. Since our goal is for every member to make Temple covenants, then the person entering the Church through baptism should know, and express a willingness to obey, the Word of Wisdom before being ordained to the Priesthood, serving in a leadership position, or receiving a full Temple Recommend. These expectations align with the 1834 decision by the First Presidency and the Kirtland and Missouri High Councils.

All men are commanded to have faith in Christ, repent of their sins, be baptized, receive the Holy Ghost, and endure to the end. This is the minimum requirement to receive a remission of sins and enter the Celestial Kingdom. All others will suffer for their own sins and be judged of a lower Kingdom. Men are not commanded to come to the Temple – that is a step the Lord invites us to take by our own will. Without commandment, we choose to take upon us the Oath and Covenant of the Priesthood and then qualify ourselves by keeping the commandment to "live by every word that proceedeth forth from the mouth of God (D&C 84: 43-44 [33-48])." The Word of Wisdom thus becomes a commandment for those that embrace the Oath and Covenant of the Priesthood by ordination and Temple covenants.

Many leaders argued that the Word of Wisdom was a commandment – and so it was for them as they were under the "Oath and Covenant of the Priesthood … to live by every word that proceedeth forth from the mouth of God." Applying the Word of Wisdom to investigators and new members as a commandment is contrary to the Lord's introductory "greeting." It is "not by commandment or constraint" and is therefore not a sin to be repented of for baptism. However, the Lord provides a transition to obedience within the Word of Wisdom. His word also "(shows) forth the <u>order</u> and will of God" (D&C 89: 1-3) for those who enter "the holiest <u>order</u> of God" (D&C 84: 18) through Priesthood ordination or Temple ordinances. As an argument for the Word of Wisdom being a commandment, President Brigham Young referenced the Oath and Covenant of the Priesthood in 1869 but appears to have applied it to all members. By baptism we qualify for the Celestial Kingdom without Word of Wisdom obedience, but by Priesthood ordination and obedience to "every word [of wisdom] … from … God" we qualify for exaltation. I call this *The Lord's Priesthood Word of Wisdom Standard.*

The poorest among men are often addicted to various substances. All are encouraged to come unto Christ and to live the Word of Wisdom. Those who are addicted to <u>legal</u> substances, but obedient to the laws of God, can be received by baptism, enjoy the fruits of Priesthood blessings and the Gift of the Holy Ghost, and prepare themselves for greater gospel opportunities by being "nourished by the good word of God" through the Addiction Recovery Program.

Those addicted to <u>illegal</u> substances could be received into the Church as <u>unbaptized associate members</u>. They also can be "nourished by the good word of God" through the Addiction Recovery Program to qualify for baptism and full membership.

"… the <u>order</u> and the will of God" refers to those who enter the "holiest <u>order</u> of God" (D&C 84: 18) under the "oath and covenant (of) the Priesthood" (D&C 84: 39 [33-48]). One does not enter this <u>order</u> by baptism, but by ordination or Temple covenants after meeting the prerequisite of baptism. The Lord "command(s)" that such are to "live by every word that proceedeth forth from the mouth of God (D&C 84: 43-44)."

The Word of Wisdom is clearly the "will of God" a Priesthood "order" holder must follow to receive the covenanted blessings, for, "In the celestial glory there are three heavens or degrees; and in order to obtain the highest, a man must enter into this <u>order</u> of the priesthood [meaning the new and everlasting covenant of marriage]; and if he does not, he cannot obtain it. He may enter into the other, but that is the end of his kingdom; he cannot have an increase (D&C 131: 1-4)."

So, the Word of Wisdom is "not by commandment or constraint," because it is not a requirement for baptism and the remission of sins. It does not keep one from the Celestial Kingdom – just exaltation within the Celestial Kingdom, which is reserved to those who enter upon the "holiest <u>order</u> of God" and follow the "commandment" to 'live by every word that proceedeth forth from the mouth of God."

Therefore, as a High Priest, the Word of Wisdom is a commandment for me, and I am now also obliged to turn away from "Anything that doth enslave (my) soul" as revealed to me by God. This willing obedience unlocks "wisdom and great treasures of knowledge, even hidden treasures (D&C 89:19)."

This understanding was clearly understood in the early Church as shown in our history. The Joseph Smith Papers have been a great blessing to us as the Church has made them available through the Internet. The administration of the Word of Wisdom is made clear through these historic records.

"In February 1834, the High Council of the Church, over which the Church Presidency presided, asked: "Whether disobedience to the word of wisdom was **a transgression** sufficient to deprive an official member from holding office in the Church, after having it sufficiently taught him?" After a free and full discussion, Joseph Smith the Prophet gave the following decision which was unanimously accepted by the council: **"No official member in this Church is worthy to hold an office after having the word of wisdom properly taught him; and he, the official member, neglecting to comply with and obey it.""**
Teachings of the Prophet Joseph Smith, Joseph Fielding Smith, p. 117 **(See APPENDIX: 1834)**

The same month, a meeting of the Missouri High Council passed a similar resolution stating that they would "not fellowship any ordained member who will or does not observe the word of Wisdom according to its litteral reading."
Minute Book 2, p. 71. Minutes, 20 Feb. 1834. **(APPENDIX: 1834)**

These decisions affected only those in the Church who would "hold an office" or were "ordained." "… disobedience … was a transgression … sufficient to deprive (a member) from … office …."

In 1837, W. A. Cowdery wrote, "Have not the authorities of the church in council assembled in this place, decided deliberately and positively, that if any official members of this church shall violate or in any wise disregard the words of wisdom which the Lord has given for the benefit of his saints, he shall lose his office?"
(See APPENDIX: 1837)

This is in keeping with an understanding that the Word of Wisdom became a commandment to all those who entered the "holiest order of God." Enforcement of the 1834 standard is evidenced by the 1838 case against the Missouri Presidency: David Whitmer, William Phelps, John Whitmer, and Oliver Cowdery.

"At a February (1838) council meeting, George Morey, a high councilor, set "forth in a very energetic manner, the proceedings of the Presidency as being iniquitous." **The four were accused of various infractions of the Word of Wisdom** and of selling their lands in Jackson County, signaling a lack of faith in the Saints' return to their promised land.

"Cowdery admitted to drinking tea three times a day for his health, and the Whitmers contended tea and coffee were not covered by the revelation. As for their property, the four threatened to leave if they were forbidden to sell their Jackson lands. Phelps said he "would move out of the accursed place." Moreover, they "would not be controlled by an ecclesiastical power of revelation whatever in their temporal concerns.""

"Considering the answers unsatisfactory, **the council removed the four from office.**"
> Taken from *Joseph Smith, Rough Stone Rolling* by Richard Lyman Bushman, 346-347. **(APPENDIX: 1838)**

In 1840 Nauvoo, Joseph Smith vigorously opposed a policy of abstinence for all Saints. After one Church Elder preached a long sermon that enjoined the Saints to "sanctity, solemnity, and temperance in the extreme, in the rigid sectarian style," Joseph reproved him for being "pharisaical and hypocritical and [for] not edifying the people." Later that evening, a Church council concluded "that a forced abstinence was not making us free but we should be under bondage with a yoak [sic] upon our necks."
(See APPENDIX: 1840 for references)

The higher standard for the Priesthood remained in place. In 1843, Twenty-two men were ordained Elders "with this express injunction, that they quit the use of tobacco and keep the Word of Wisdom."
> Historian's Office, JS History, Draft Notes, 10 Apr. 1843.
> **(See APPENDIX: 1843)**

"... compl(iance) with" the Word of Wisdom would have included proscriptions against "Tobacco", "wine or strong drink", "hot drinks" (clarified as Tea and Coffee by both Joseph and Hyrum Smith, omitting Chocolate which was also a popular hot drink of the day), and "flesh also of beasts and of the fowls ... (which) are to be used sparingly ... only in times of winter, or of cold, or famine." Little historic reference is found about eating meat sparingly, although Hyrum Smith spoke of the Lord's concern about killing animals needlessly.

Brigham Young, who preached against "swine meat" **(See APPENDIX: 1868)** was critical of Hyrum Smith's observance:

> "In February 1860, Brigham Young admitted to a close group of confidantes, that he found Hyrum Smith's position on the Word of Wisdom incongruous.
> "Hyrum would eat about three lb of fat pork in a day," Brigham noted incredulously, "and yet be so severe upon a tobacco chewer." [Here Brigham is likely referring to himself.]"
>> Brigham Young Office Journal, February 24, 1860, Book D, August 8, 1858 to September 30, 1863.
>> From Paul H. Peterson and Ronald W. Walker, "Brigham Young's Word of Wisdom Legacy," BYU Studies, vol. 42, nos. 3–4 (2003), 29–64. Note 118. **(See APPENDIX:1860)**

Obedience to the Word of Wisdom was not required for baptism and membership in the Church under the Prophet Joseph Smith. This is consistent with the Word of Wisdom being "sent greeting; not by commandment … showing forth the … will of God in the temporal salvation of all saints" rather than a commandment for the spiritual or eternal salvation of the saints. The High Council at Kirtland understood disobedience to the Word of Wisdom to be a "transgression" rather than a sin. Since baptism is for the remission of sins, it held that obedience to the Word of Wisdom was not required for baptism. This same standard/decision could apply to new members today.

This action is also appropriate considering the revelation received in the previous year detailing the Oath and Covenant of the Priesthood. Those obtaining the Priesthood (or temple covenants associated with the Oath and Covenant of the Priesthood) are commanded to "live by every word that proceedeth forth from the mouth of God" (D&C 84:43-44). They would not qualify for Priesthood ordination or leadership positions in the Church until they were compliant with the Word of Wisdom which was recognized as the "will of God" for any Priesthood holder. It is also important for us to realize that observance of the Word of Wisdom in the days of Joseph Smith and Brigham Young was tempered by medicinal use that was very often self-prescribed. The proscribed items of the Word of Wisdom were also considered to have medicinal uses, particularly tea and alcohol.

Leaders and members alike felt it alright to use these substances during time of illness or "need." For example, during the building up of Nauvoo, the members were plagued with malaria. Joseph is reported to have told members to "make tea and drink it" when river water was unsuitable. He "often made tea and administered it with his own hands." He is also recorded to have drunk wine and beer on occasion.

See *Saints, Vol 1., 1815-1846, The Standard of Truth*, Chapter 15, note 27. http://www.josephsmithpapers.org/paper-summary/revelation-27-february-1833-dc-89/1#historical-intro

So, we see that obedience to the Word of Wisdom was considered a commandment to those who were under the Oath and Covenant of the Priesthood with an allowance for medicinal use in times of need. However, for those investigating the Church and for new members, the Word of Wisdom was not a commandment – as the Lord states – but it was still "the will of God" they were invited to follow, especially if they intended to enter the "holiest order of God."

CHAPTER TWO

<u>A PERIOD OF SIN AND CONFUSION</u>
(Brigham Young to Heber J. Grant)

The Prophet Brigham Young

Have we failed to understand the difference between the investigator and new member, and the Priesthood holder when it comes to the Word of Wisdom? Except for the Prophet Joseph, the history of Word of Wisdom advocacy, adherence, and administration, shows a lack of understanding the Lord's words.

Following the death of the Prophet Joseph Smith, the Lord brought the Church west under the leadership of the Prophet Brigham Young. Historical records show that during that period, he resumed his practice of chewing Tobacco **(See APPENDIX: 1847).** It was an earlier addiction that drew the attention of Hyrum Smith to Brigham Young's chagrin **(See APPENDIX: 1868).** As President of the Twelve Apostles, he must have become obedient during Joseph's tenure as Prophet, given that other senior leaders were released for not following the Word of Wisdom **(See APPENDIX: 1838).** Later President Young repented of his departure from the Priesthood standard and by the time the Saint George Temple was dedicated he was "just right" with the Lord **(See APPENDIX: 1877).** This repentance seems to have begun in earnest in 1851. Perhaps motivated by personal guilt, he appears to have wanted his repentance to apply to the entire Church.

In *Answers to Gospel Questions, 1: 197,* Joseph Fielding Smith answers the following question:

> "Will you please tell me if the Word of Wisdom has ever been presented to the Church as a commandment making its observation obligatory upon the members of the Church?"

He answers:

> "The simple answer to this question is yes, such commandment has been given and repeated on several occasions. September 9, 1851, President Brigham Young stated that the members of the Church had had sufficient time to be taught the import of this revelation and that henceforth it was to be considered a divine commandment. This was first put to vote before the female members of the congregation and then before the men and by unanimous vote accepted. President Joseph F. Smith at a conference meeting in October 1908, made the same statement, and this has been repeated from time to time."

The 1851 Conference action by Brigham Young **(See APPENDIX: 1851)** to place the women and then the men (under 90) under covenant to keep all the prohibitions of the Word of Wisdom is often cited as him declaring it to be a commandment for all members of the Church, not just leaders, yet we do not find the word "commandment" anywhere in the **"Minutes of the General Conference."** The members present "covenant(ed) to leave off the use of tobacco, whisky, and all things mentioned in the Word of Wisdom." (http://contentdm.lib.byu.edu/utils/getfile/collection/ MStar/id/37435/filename/37436.pdf).

> "The Patriarch [**John Smith**] again rose to speak on the Word of Wisdom, and urging on the brethren to leave off using tobacco, &c.

> "President Young rose to put the motion and called on all the sisters who will leave off the use of tea, coffee, &c., to manifest it by raising the right hand; seconded and carried.

> "And then put the following motion; calling on all the boys [*sic*] who were under ninety years of age who would **covenant to leave off the use of tobacco, whisky, and <u>all things mentioned</u> in the Word of Wisdom,** to manifest it in the same manner, which was carried unanimously."

> "The Patriarch then said, may the Lord bless you and help you to keep all your covenants. Amen.

> "President Young amongst other things said he knew the goodness of the people, and the Lord bears with our weakness; we must serve the Lord, and those who go with me will keep the Word of Wisdom, and if the High Priests, the Seventies, the Elders, and others will not serve the Lord, we will sever them from the Church. I will draw the line, and know who is for the Lord and who is not, and those who will not keep the Word of Wisdom, I will cut off from the Church; I throw out a challenge to all men and women."[32]

> **"Minutes of the General Conference"**, Tuesday, Sep. 9, 1851, afternoon session *Millennial Star*, 1 February 1852, vol. 14, p. 35. Taken from Wikipedia: Word of Wisdom https://en.wikipedia.org/wiki/Word_of_Wisdom#Emphasize d_by_Brigham_Young

From Paul H. Peterson and Ronald W. Walker, *Brigham Young's Word of Wisdom Legacy*, BYU Studies, vol. 42, nos. 3–4 (2003), 29–64:

"The September 1851 Conference in Review. Church leaders would later refer to the September 1851 conference as the point in time when Joseph Smith's revelation was accepted by the members of the Church as a binding commandment." [46]

46 For instance, see Francis M. Lyman, in Seventy-Ninth Annual Conference of The Church of Jesus Christ of Latter-day Saints (Salt Lake City: The Church of Jesus Christ of Latter-day Saints, 1908), 55; and McCue, "Did the Word of Wisdom Become a Commandment in 1851?" 66–77.

See Joseph Fielding Smith, Improvement Era 59 (February 1956): 78. This influential article responded to this question: Has the Word of Wisdom "ever been presented to the Church as a commandment making its observance obligatory upon the members of the Church?" To this inquiry, Elder Smith replied, "The simple answer to this question is yes, such commandment has been given and repeated on several occasions. [On] September 9, 1851, President Brigham Young stated that the members of the Church had had sufficient time to be taught the import of this revelation and that henceforth it was to be considered a divine commandment." Elder Smith's statement was later quoted in various books, Church Sunday School manuals, and seminary and institute manuals. The most recent reference to the supposedly pivotal 1851 conference action was made by President Ezra Taft Benson in his address to the April 1983 general conference. Ezra Taft Benson, "A Principle with a Promise," Ensign 13 (May 1983): 53.

"However, little evidence exists that Brigham himself regarded this September conference as a pivotal event in Word of Wisdom reform. Certainly, he took no steps, then or later, to make full compliance a membership test for either Church leaders or the members in general. [47]

> 47 When the city's bishops met at their regular coordinating meeting in October 1851, there was telling uncertainty about the recent Word of Wisdom counsel. Had the recent conference made the health code "a Law in Israel?" asked one of the bishops. Presiding Bishop Edward Hunter ended the meeting's discussion by saying that "as for making . . . [the Word of Wisdom] a Test of fellowship he could not at present decide."
>
> > Record of Bishops' Meetings, October 12, 1851, "Report of Wards, Ordinations, Instructions, and General Proceedings of the Bishops and Lesser Priesthood," Church Archives.

"And there is no record of other Church leaders in President Young's lifetime using the 1851 September conference as a text. In short, the Saints seemed to have understood that while "Brother Brigham" had taken a firm stance on obeying the revelation, his celebrated (and often exaggerated) pulpit language—in this case using the threat of excommunication for non-observers—reached beyond his actual policy."

Thomas G. Alexander, in *Mormonism in Transition,* states:

"Although Brigham Young declared the Word of Wisdom to be a commandment and secured the approval of some of the Saints to that proposition, **he announced no revelation on the subject, and actual observance did not coincide with the public pronouncement. An 1851 conference and in some cases other conference addresses or reminiscences of addresses are often cited as the date the Word of Wisdom became binding as a commandment.**

"However, during Brigham Young's lifetime, after the conference, he and other Church leaders and members failed to observe the Word of Wisdom as we interpret it today. Brigham Young and other Church leaders again reemphasized the Word of Wisdom in the late 1860s and early 1870s, but this reemphasis seems to have been more closely related to the larger effort to discourage imports than to emphasize the health aspects of the principle. From the death of Brigham Young until after the turn of the century, adherence was intermittent. In 1883 and 1884 the general authorities, following the lead of President John Taylor, emphasized the need to adhere to the Word of Wisdom. Thereafter, it seems generally to have laid dormant." 4

> 4. Peterson, "Word of Wisdom", 55–79; Robert J. McCue, "Did the Word of Wisdom Become a Commandment in 1851?" 66–77; Leonard J. Arrington, "An Economic Interpretation of the Word of Wisdom," 47. **Some of those making statements remembering Brigham Young's declaration that the Word of Wisdom was a commandment included John Taylor in 1853 and Joseph F. Smith in 1909. It seems quite clear, however, that the principle was not generally regarded in the same way as it is today—that is, as essential for holding responsible positions in the Church or for participating in temple ordinances."**

In 1860, Brigham Young offered counsel on chewing tobacco and did not charge those using it with sin:

> "In 1860 he (Brigham Young) said, "Many of the brethren chew tobacco, and I have advised them to be modest about it...Do not glory in this disgraceful practice. If you must use tobacco, **put a small portion in your mouth when no person sees you, and be careful that no one sees you chew it. I do not charge you with sin**. You have the 'Word of Wisdom.' Read it...It is, at least, disgraceful to you to expose your absurdities" (JD 8:362)."

> **http://en.wikisource.org/w/index.php?title=Journal_of_ Discourses/Volume_8/Confession_of_Faults%2C_%26 c.&oldid=625921**). http://www.somemormonstuff.com/the-word-of-wisdom/ **(See APPENDIX: 1860)**

How could this statement be made if Brigham Young or the Lord declared the Word of Wisdom a commandment in 1851? The statement is like concerns over the "appearance of evil" that judges those using electronic cigarettes, but unlike Brigham Young, many of today's observers do consider electronic cigarettes to be sin because of the pre-Dec-2020-Handbook's open-ended proscriptions.

By his own public record, Brigham Young did not keep the 1851 covenant until 1860 and acknowledged in 1869 that the Word of Wisdom was not a commandment. **(See APPENDIX: 1860 and 1869)** Placing the leaders of the Church under covenant might have been more appropriate given the Prophet Joseph's 1834 decision. Leaders could then have set an example for members.

The covenant included "leav(ing) off … all things mentioned in the Word of Wisdom." If this is when the Word of Wisdom became a commandment, then we are now also under commandment to eat meat sparingly.

If Brigham Young did excommunicate violators of the Word of Wisdom, that practice soon stopped since senior leaders continued to violate it up until 1921. If leaders had been put under covenant, they could have simply been released for non-observance. By his own public admission, President Brigham Young did not stop chewing tobacco, and drinking tea and coffee, until 1860, nine years after leading the Conference vote to "covenant to leave off the use of tobacco, whisky, and all things mentioned in the Word of Wisdom." Who was to excommunicate Brigham Young, or release him for non-observance? Members are not excommunicated for violating the Word of Wisdom today, but they are typically released from leadership positions and do not receive Temple Recommends, which is more consistent with the Lord's standard practiced by the Prophet Joseph Smith.

John Taylor and Joseph F. Smith both reported hearing Brigham Young refer to the Word of Wisdom as a commandment. Did the Lord declare this to Brigham Young? He did not claim so. Succeeding leaders of the Church have also not claimed the voice of the Lord declaring the Word of Wisdom a commandment. All have harkened back to 1851, overturning the Lord's 1833 statement in their lack of understanding.

"Late in his Presidency (1869) Brigham Young referenced "the oath and covenant (of) the priesthood" (D&C 84: 39, 43-44), but seemed to apply the requirement of obedience to all members, just as in his previous statements and the 1851 Church conference vote. **"I know that some say the revelations upon these (Word of Wisdom) points are not given by way of commandment. <u>Very well</u>, but we are commanded to observe every word that proceeds from the mouth of God.""**

(Young, Brigham. *Discourses of Brigham Young.* Selected by John A. Widtsoe. 1941. pgs, 182-33) **(See APPENDIX 1869)**

The 1834 decision of the First Presidency and Kirtland High Council, that "No official member in this Church is worthy to hold an office after having the word of wisdom properly taught him; and he, the official member, neglecting to comply with and obey it" is not highlighted by Church leaders, nor is Joseph Smith's requirement for obedience to the Word of Wisdom for ordination to the Melchizedek Priesthood. This may be because it was limited to "office" holders, and many high office holders prior to 1921 did not strictly follow the Word of Wisdom. This was also true after President Brigham Young's Church vote in 1851, many leaders still did not strictly follow the Word of Wisdom. It may also be because the standard is now applied to all members and one cannot be received by baptism into the Church without a commitment to be obedient to the Word of Wisdom.

The Church has not offered the Oath and Covenant of the Priesthood to provide an explanation for "<u>not by commandment or constraint</u>, but ... the <u>order</u> and <u>will of God</u>." Following Joseph Smith, the history of the Word of Wisdom, and the struggle of Church leaders to administer it, suggests that they did not understand this principle. The Church states, without a confirming revelation, that the Word of Wisdom is a commandment while the word of the Lord in the Word of Wisdom remains "not by commandment or constraint." The word of the Lord is clear and no new direct revelation from the Lord has been reported to modify the Word of Wisdom. What history shows is confusion in the ranks even at the highest levels. The Joseph Smith standard for those under the Oath and Covenant of the Priesthood, has not been followed since his martyrdom.

The confusion in the leadership ranks is illustrated by this record:

> "THE STATUS OF THE WORD OF WISDOM at the turn of the century is evident from contemporary sources. At a meeting on May 5,1898, the First Presidency and Twelve discussed the Word of Wisdom. One member read from the twelfth volume of the Journal of Discourses a statement by Brigham Young that seemed to support the notion that the Word of Wisdom was a commandment of God. **Lorenzo Snow, then President of the Council of the Twelve** agreed, saying that he believed the Word of Wisdom was a commandment and that it should be carried out to the letter. In doing so, he **said, members should be taught to refrain from eating meat except in dire necessity, because Joseph Smith had taught that animals have spirits. Wilford Woodruff, then President of the Church, said he looked upon the Word of Wisdom as a commandment and that all members should observe it, but for the present, no definite action should be taken except that the members should be taught to refrain from meat.** The minutes of the meeting record that **"President Woodruff said he regarded the Word of Wisdom in its entirety as given of the Lord for the Latter-day Saints to observe, but he did not think that Bishops should withhold recommends from persons who did not adhere strictly to it."**
>
> Diary of Heber J. Grant, May 5, and June 30, 1898, LDS Church Archives; "Journal History of the Church of Jesus Christ of Latter-day Saints" (JH), May 5, 1898, LDS Church **(See APPENDIX: 1898)**

It is often said today that the Word of Wisdom was not originally given as a commandment because it would have immediately made many members sinners. This rationale comes from President Joseph F. Smith's 1913 statement:

"The reason undoubtedly why the Word of Wisdom was given—as not by 'commandment or restraint' was that at that time, at least, if it had been given as a commandment it would have brought every man, addicted to the use of these noxious things, under condemnation; so the Lord was merciful and gave them a chance to overcome, before He brought them under the law."

President Joseph F. Smith, *Conference Report* (October 1913), 14. **(See APPENDIX: 1913)**

Two questions arise from this statement:
1. When did the Lord bring "them under the law"? The Prophet Joseph did bring <u>leaders</u> under the law in 1834 and many early members were reported following the Word of Wisdom exactly!
2. What of new members who enter the Church with addictions; would not "the Lord (be) merciful and g(i)ve them a chance to overcome, before He brought them under the law"?

President Joseph F. Smith was understanding the Lord's mercy but was failing to recognize the transition the Lord had already provided for every person in "not by commandment or constraint" at first, but "showing forth the order and will of God" as the new member embraced the Oath and Covenant of the Priesthood.

Placing the leaders of the Church under covenant might have been a more appropriate action in 1851, given the Prophet Joseph's 1834 decision. Leaders could then have set an example for all members.

The Lord's leadership standard as understood and practiced by the Prophet Joseph Smith was not strictly upheld by many senior leaders until President Heber J. Grant established the Word of Wisdom standard for a Temple Recommend in 1921. At some undetermined point, perhaps in or shortly after 1930, leaders went beyond the leadership standard and applied a <u>reduced standard</u> to <u>all members</u> – eating meat sparingly has not been followed. **(See APPENDIX: 1921 and 1930)**

CHAPTER THREE

A REDUCED AND IMPOSED STANDARD FOR ALL SAINTS
(Heber J. Grant to present)

The Prophet Heber J. Grant

In 1921, President Heber J Grant made obedience to the Word of Wisdom a requirement for a Temple Recommend. President Grant required obedience to the prohibitions on Tobacco and "intoxicating drinks." Sources are conflicted as to whether Tea and Coffee were included in that decision. Heber J. Grant in January 1930 warned bishops that men using tobacco were not to be called on missions.

Of this decision, the Church website says:

> "In 1921, the Lord inspired President Heber J. Grant to call on all Saints to live the Word of Wisdom to the letter by completely abstaining from all alcohol, coffee, tea, and tobacco. Today Church members are expected to live this higher standard."17

> 17 Moderation rather than abstinence was applied to virtually all of the "do nots" of the Word of Wisdom until the early 20th century. On the tightening up of Word of Wisdom observance, see Thomas G. Alexander, Mormonism in Transition: A History of the Latter-day Saints, 1890–1930 (Urbana: University of Illinois Press, 1986), 258–71; Paul H. Peterson and Ronald W. Walker, "Brigham Young's Word of Wisdom Legacy," BYU Studies, vol. 42, nos. 3–4 (2003), 29–64. https://history.lds.org/article/doctrine-and-covenants-word-of-wisdom?lang=eng

The reference cited by the Church states:

> "After the inauguration of Heber J. Grant's administration in 1918, however, the advice became less flexible. In 1921, church leadership made adherence to the Word of Wisdom a requirement for admission to the temple. Before this stake presidents and bishops had been encouraged to in this matter, but exceptions had been made. Apparently under this new emphasis, in March, 1921, George F. Richards, both as apostle and president of the Salt Lake Temple, phoned two Salt Lake City bishops about two tobacco users who had come to the temple and told the bishops "to try to clean them up before they come here again.""15
>
> 15 George F. Richards Journal, March 26, 1921. Information on the Temple recommend bookfrom K. Heybron Adams, formerly of the LDS Church Archives. Thomas G. Alexander, Mormonism in Transition: A History of the Latter-day Saints, 1890–1930

In the process of conducting this research, I felt the Spirit's witness that President Heber J. Grant was correct in understanding the Lord's will that the Word of Wisdom (D&C 89) be followed by those entering upon Temple Covenants. Such individuals are under the Oath and Covenant of the Priesthood's commandment to "live by every word that proceedeth forth from the mouth of God." (D&C 84: 43-44) I have not been able to find any record of this decision or letter. Was there any revelation cited? Did it apply strictly to those seeking a Temple Recommend or to "all saints" as the Church website suggests? Rather than being a new policy, this action took a closer step towards Joseph Smith's requirement that all leaders be obedient to the Word of Wisdom. Men and women who make Temple covenants, are under the "holiest _order_ of God" standard, so these actions began to restore the Lord's Word of Wisdom standard as followed by the Prophet Joseph Smith.

The Church then changed the Lord's words from "not by commandment or constraint" to commandment for all. When did the Church decide that obedience to the Word of Wisdom was a requirement for baptism into the Church? I have not been able to determine this but suspect that it occurred around 1930 or shortly thereafter. Since missionaries prior to 1930 were not required to live the Word of Wisdom, it is reasonable to assert that obedience to the Word of Wisdom was not required for converts. That may have changed when President Grant made this change in the requirements for serving as a missionary. Certainly by 1955, when my father was baptized, he was required to stop smoking and drinking alcohol. Records for this period are very scant or were not made available to historians whose works I accessed. I have not located any letters from the First Presidency detailing these changes in Word of Wisdom policy.

When I served as a missionary in the Philippines from 1968-1970, we required obedience to the Word of Wisdom for baptism.

Proscriptions today omit "flesh also of beasts and of the fowls...." It is rarely emphasized and is a major contributor to many "Western" diseases, thus having a negative effect on "the temporal salvation of (many) saints." Presidents Brigham Young, Lorenzo Snow, and Wilford Woodruff sought to restrict meat, but President Joseph F. Smith dropped the emphasis. This changing emphasis again highlights a lack of direct revelation on the topic, or a failure to understand and apply the original revelation from the Lord.

CHAPTER FOUR

THE LORD'S WILL FOR CONSUMING THE FLESH OF ANIMALS AND BIRDS

When Adam and Eve were placed in the Garden of Eden, they were not given the flesh of animals to eat.

> "And God said, Behold, I have given you every herb bearing seed, which is upon the face of all the earth, and every tree, in the which is the fruit of a tree yielding seed; to you it shall be for meat. And to every beast of the earth, and to every fowl of the air, and to every thing that creepeth upon the earth, wherein there is life, I have given every green herb for meat: and it was so." (Genesis 1: 29-30 See also Moses 2:29, and Abraham 4:29)

It is after the Flood that we first see God mention flesh for "meat."

> "The first (scriptural) mention of animal flesh as a source of food is the Lord's instruction to Noah after the Flood subsided and he and his family left the ark. God had given Adam and Eve herbs and fruit for meat (Genesis 1:29), but now God tells Noah *"every moving thing that liveth shall be for meat" (Genesis 9:3)*. Joseph Smith added a qualification to this injunction in 1830, three years before the Word of Wisdom was revealed:

> > *"And surely, blood shall not be shed, only for meat, to save your lives; and the blood of every beast will I require at your hand. (JST Genesis 9:11)*

> "The following year, in a revelation given in May 1831, Joseph Smith warned that while the flesh of animals is ordained for the use of man, "wo be unto man that sheddeth blood or that wasteth flesh and hath no need" (D&C 49:21)."
> > https://www.mormoninterpreter.com/getting-into-the-meat-of-the-word-of-wisdom/

These scriptures provide an understanding of what God means by "flesh also of beasts and of the fowls … are to be used sparingly." This has much more to do with respect for life, than for diet considerations. My father loved to hunt deer in New Zealand. Not long after joining the Church he saw the life drain out of a stag he shot and decided to give up the practice since meat was readily available in smaller quantities through grocery stores. The significance of the animal's life had affected him.

The product of the beasts and fowl (milk, cheese, and eggs) are not proscribed, and they offer high quality protein, vitamins, and essential amino acids that the human body needs. Therefore, the dietary benefits of beasts and fowl can be derived without their killing; nevertheless, the Lord allows for the "flesh also of beasts and of the fowls … to be used sparingly; … only in times of winter, or of cold, or famine … and excess of hunger."

The Lord also makes clear that forbidding to eat meat "is not ordained of God," but that shedding "blood (and wasting) flesh" of "beasts … and the fowls" when there is "no need" is not appropriate.

> "And whoso forbiddeth (biddeth in the footnote) to abstain from meats, that man should not eat the same, is not ordained of God; for, behold, <u>the beasts of the field and the fowls of the air</u>, and that which cometh of the earth, <u>is ordained for the use of man for food</u> and for raiment, and that he might have in abundance. <u>And wo be unto man that sheddeth blood or that wasteth flesh and hath no need</u>." (D&C 49: 18-19, 21)

It is clear then that the Word of Wisdom is not vegetarianism (no animal, bird, or fish meat), nor is it veganism (vegetarianism plus no animal products such as milk, cheese, or eggs). Fish is not proscribed in the Word of Wisdom, and we know that the Lord consumed fish.

The use of "beast and fowl" meat in times of "winter" is obviously seasonal, but "cold" can be night and early morning, "famine and excess of hunger" can be measured daily and have much to do with the stability of the society in which one lives. Those living in the higher latitudes and altitudes will also find themselves relying more on animal products and flesh because of the cold.

The way that the Lord fed the Israelites in the deserts of Sinai and Arabia is instructive. Quail flew into the camp in the early evening and manna fell upon the ground in the morning (Exodus 16: 11-15). Consumption of the Quail meat provided a slow release of energy that lasted the long, very cold, nights. We experienced the cold of desert nights when we camped out near Jabal Musa (the Mount of Moses) in northern Arabia. However, when the people lusted for flesh, the Lord was angry and plagued them with the Quail (Numbers 11). Thus, we get a sense of the Lord's measured use of meat.

When our family moved from Hawaii to Alaska for a new military assignment, I continued to eat a cereal and fruit breakfast for a short while until I realized a need to change my diet for the colder climate. After an hour or two I was typically starving. A switch to bacon and eggs solved the problem very nicely.

Each will judge what "sparingly" means for flesh of beast and fowl. The loss of half my kidney function due to kidney stones brought me to a definition of "sparingly." My Nephrologist restricted me to 80g of protein per day to prevent further kidney damage. The 80g is a total of all protein (plant/animal/fish sources) that applies to anyone to reduce kidney damage, but I was stunned to learn that more than 80g of "beast and fowl" flesh protein is even worse, because the incidence of kidney stones goes up dramatically in that case. The Lord's council to eat meat sparingly took on a quantitative value for me – I stay well under 80g per day because of the other proteins in my diet from grains, nuts, eggs, and fish.

CHAPTER FIVE

<u>THE GENERAL HANDBOOK AND THE ROLE OF REVELATION</u>
(How President Nelson's December 2020 Handbook has
changed Word of Wisdom administration for the better)

The Prophet Russell M. Nelson

Up until December 2020, the General Handbook statements and policies about the Word of Wisdom went unchanged from at least 2010. The December 2020 Handbook has significantly changed Church policy in a very positive and simplified way. The negative effects of the earlier Handbook will be discussed first.

A. 2010 to pre-December-2020 Word of Wisdom Policy

In the Handbooks prior to Dec 2020, the Church continued a multiplicity of proscriptions from at least 2010 that required members using any harmful or habit-forming substances to be "under the care of a competent physician."

> 38.7.13   Word of Wisdom
>
> "The only official interpretation of "hot drinks" (D&C 89:9) in the Word of Wisdom is the statement made by early Church leaders that the term "hot drinks" means tea and coffee.
>
> "Members should not use any substance that contains illegal drugs. Nor should members use harmful or habit-forming substances except under the care of a competent physician."

The definition of "hot drinks" is consistent with clarifications by both Joseph and Hyrum Smith.

Use of "illegal drugs" is a sin against the laws of the land. They are obviously harmful to the body but were not listed as proscriptions in the Word of Wisdom given by the Lord (D&C 89). All of the proscriptions the Lord listed were lawful and common.

The final sentence added significant proscriptions to the Word of Wisdom – well beyond that listed by the Lord in the only direct revelation He has provided. "Nor should members use <u>harmful **or** habit-forming</u> substances …." Examples include:
1. Electronic cigarettes
2. Marijuana
3. Opioids
4. Caffeine
5. Excessive meat consumption leading to disease
6. Sugar (in foods and drinks) leading to disease
7. Refined carbohydrates leading to disease
8. And many more ….

Such "harmful or habit-forming substances," if consumed, must also be managed "under the care of a competent physician." This placed a significant financial burden on members struggling with these addictions. The rule was so broad that it appeared to be largely ignored, except for members who got doctor notes to be excused for using substances their bishops were concerned about.

No provision was offered for members with addiction problems to attend the free Addiction Recovery Program Meetings under the care of their Bishop.

No direct revelation was cited for proscriptions against "harmful or habit-forming substances." However, the Lord's word to me shows His concern for "Anything that doth enslave the soul of man …."

Excessive meat consumption is medically linked to "Western" diseases. It is listed as a proscription by the Lord in the Word of Wisdom but is not emphasized by the Church. Might it have been better to follow the Lord in limiting meat consumption rather than opening the Word of Wisdom to a long and unspecified list of "harmful or habit-forming substances (under) the care of a competent physician"?

The Word of Wisdom baptism interview question for investigators applying for baptism was: "You have been taught that membership in The Church of Jesus Christ of Latter-day Saints includes living gospel standards. What do you understand about the following standards? Are you willing to obey them? … The Word of Wisdom" (General Handbook 38.2.3.3.). "Are you willing to obey …" indicates that a convert is not technically required to be obedient at time of baptism but the concept that the Word of Wisdom is a commandment for all members is implied in the expected standard of conduct for members.

For a Temple Recommend the Word of Wisdom question was simply "Do you understand and obey the Word of Wisdom?" It was open to interpretation without specific proscriptions being listed. Some individuals obtained recommends who used electronic cigarettes and legal Marijuana, while others would not be depending on how Mission Presidents, Bishops, and Stake Presidents interpreted the Word of Wisdom and enforced the General Handbook.

Caffeine is certainly "habit forming" yet Church statements about it were in conflict with the Handbook. The Salt Lake Tribune found "the LDS Church posted a statement on its website saying that "the church does not prohibit the use of caffeine" and … A day later, the website wording was slightly softened, saying only that "the church revelation spelling out health practices ... does not mention the use of caffeine.""
[https://archive.sltrib.com/article.php?id=54797595&itype=cmsid]

This was an interesting statement for two reasons:

1. "the church revelation" indicates only one – D&C 89.
2. Church Word of Wisdom policy is not "revelation."

So, what was a member to do?

Sugars and refined carbohydrates were generally ignored in policy and often lead to obesity, yet obese candidates for baptism or a Temple Recommend went unchallenged. On the other hand, individuals who used electronic cigarettes were denied recommends based on the "appearance of evil." Why not the obese?

The Handbook's statement proscribing "harmful or habit-forming substances except under the care of a competent physician" probably qualified as "pharisaical and hypocritical" in the eyes of the Prophet Joseph Smith.

On 15 August 2019, an Official Church Statement on the Word of Wisdom, added more "prohibited" items:

> "The Word of Wisdom is a law of health for the physical and spiritual benefit of God's children. It includes instruction about what foods are good for us and those substances to avoid. Over time, Church leaders have provided additional instruction on those things that are encouraged or forbidden by the Word of Wisdom, and have taught that substances that are destructive, habit-forming or addictive should be avoided.

"In recent publications for Church members, Church leaders
have clarified that several substances are prohibited by the
Word of Wisdom, including vaping or e-cigarettes, green tea,
and coffee-based products. They also have cautioned that
substances such as marijuana and opioids should be used
only for medicinal purposes as prescribed by a competent
physician."
> https://newsroom.churchofjesuschrist.org/article/statement
> -word-of-wisdom-august-2019

Once again, no revelation from God expanding the "not" for man list
in D&C 89 was cited. Then in December 2020 a stunning reversal
occurred – the Church returned to the Lord's "not" list – "tobacco,
strong drinks (alcohol), and hot drinks (tea and coffee)".

B. The December 2020 Word of Wisdom Policy

President Russell M. Nelson's update to the Word of Wisdom in
December 2020 removes the additional restrictions that could only
be used "under the care of a competent physician" completely,
except for marijuana under medical permission.

The clear implication is that the stunning list of additional
prohibitions that had burdened Church members and restrained
investigators, had not been received by revelation, but were
probably the "best" intentions of Church leaders.

Also, this new policy on the Word of Wisdom overrules the 15
August 2019 Official Church Statement by its currency – previous
policy statements are consolidated or removed by the Handbook
update. Hence the vaping, green tea, and coffee products policy is
gone except for hot green tea. The Lord's "hot drinks" was defined
by the Prophet Joseph Smith to include hot tea, which is green tea.

The Handbook now states:

38.7.13.

"(God) revealed (the Word of Wisdom) for the physical and
spiritual benefit of His children. Prophets have clarified that
the teachings in Doctrine and Covenants 89 include
<u>abstinence from</u> tobacco, strong drinks (alcohol), and hot
drinks (tea and coffee).

"Prophets have also taught members to <u>avoid </u>substances that are harmful, illegal, or addictive or that impair judgment.

"There are other harmful substances and practices that are not specified in the Word of Wisdom or by Church leaders. Members should <u>use wisdom and prayerful judgment</u> in making choices to promote their physical, spiritual, and emotional health.

"The Apostle Paul stated: "Know ye not that your body is the temple of the Holy Ghost which is in you, which ye have of God, and ye are not your own? For ye are bought with a price: therefore glorify God in your body, and in your spirit, which are God's" (1 Corinthians 6:19–20).

"The Lord promises spiritual and temporal blessings to those who obey the Word of Wisdom and the guidance of living prophets (see Doctrine and Covenants 89:18–21)."

… and for Medical Marijuana:

38.7.9

"<u>The Church opposes the use of marijuana for non-medical purposes</u>. See "Word of Wisdom and Healthy Practices" (38.7.13).

"However, marijuana may be used for medicinal purposes when the following conditions are met:

> "The use is determined to be medically necessary by a licensed physician or another legally approved medical provider.

> "The person follows the dosage and mode of administration from the physician or other authorized medical provider. The Church does not approve of vaping marijuana unless the medical provider has authorized it based on medical necessity.

"The Church does not approve of smoking marijuana, including for medical purposes."

Note that the only "abstinence" is tobacco, alcohol, hot tea and hot coffee. All of the "should not use" restrictions "except under the care of a competent physician" are gone except for marijuana. With that exception all other harmful substances are for "members to avoid" – they are no longer restrictive as "should not use" or "prohibited." Therefore "vaping or e-cigarettes" is in this category as also "coffee-based products" and mild "green tea" drinks. Hot "green tea" is still an abstinence product since all tea is green tea (processed or not) – to be discussed in the next chapter.

However, the Church still insists in the first sentence of the new policy, "The Word of Wisdom is a commandment of God" (Handbook 38.7.13) while the only claimed revelation from the Lord states it is "not by commandment or constraint" (D&C 89: 2) and Church claims that the Word of Wisdom became a commandment in 1851 under President Brigham Young are not supported by the historic record. It is certainly true that the Word of Wisdom is a commandment for those under the Oath and Covenant of the Priesthood.

Members are not excommunicated for violating the Word of Wisdom today, but they are typically released from leadership positions and do not receive Temple Recommends, which is more consistent with Joseph Smith's decision on an obedience standard based on the Lord's proscribed items for Priesthood and leaders. What would the Lord's standard as applied by Joseph Smith look like today?

It appears that we as a Church have tended to ignore the reality that we have not faithfully upheld and lived the Word of Wisdom. Following the death of the Prophet Joseph Smith, the Prophet Brigham Young led the Church into the west and established it in the safety of the mountains, but he also gave in to his personal weaknesses of chewing tobacco and drinking tea and coffee. In his efforts to repent he incorrectly sought to apply the Word of Wisdom to all members by using the Oath and Covenant of the Priesthood which is binding only upon those under that covenant. While violating the Lord's and Joseph Smith's leadership standard, he sought to apply that standard to all.

This has been true of many of the prophets that followed as they debated amongst themselves whether the Word of Wisdom was a commandment or not. The claim that the Word of Wisdom became a commandment for all members in 1851 is simply false. Sadly, it certainly was a commandment for Brigham Young and other leaders. He and many other leaders were in need of repentance. Even today the Lord's proscription of meat receives little emphasis from the leadership. Our Word of Wisdom history has been one of obedience under the Prophet Joseph Smith, sin from Brigham Young through Joseph F. Smith, and imposition since Heber J. Grant.

While many leaders and members have faithfully applied the Word of Wisdom in their lives, I believe it is time for the Church to restore the Lord's administrative guideline to the Word of Wisdom:

> "sent greeting; not by commandment or constraint, but by revelation and the word of wisdom, showing forth the order and will of God in the temporal salvation of all saints in the last days." (D&C 89:2)

Expecting all members of the Church to be obedient to the Word of Wisdom today is discouraging to many of God's children that are in need of recovery from addiction. They need to be acceptable for baptism and have access to the Gift of the Holy Ghost by the standard the Lord declared: "sent [by] greeting; not by commandment or constraint."

The encouragement we have all received from the prophets is most certainly true: "Know ye not that ye are the temple of God, and that the Spirit of God dwelleth in you? If any man defile the temple of God, him shall God destroy; for the temple of God is holy, which temple ye are." (1 Corinthians 3: 16-17) When we defile our bodies with harmful and addictive substances, the natural order God established generally leads to an earlier demise.

The role revelation has played throughout this history of Word of Wisdom application and the Church Handbooks is addressed by Roy W. Doxey, and Thomas G. Alexander. The prophets have also addressed it in that there has been no claim to new direct revelation from the Lord. Inspirational guidance seems to have been the norm with outside influences such as Utah State politics and US national movements against alcohol and Tobacco playing a role.

"… What role did revelation play in the matter? **It is clear that Section 89 of the Doctrine and Covenants was given as a revelation to Joseph Smith.** Advice that the members of the Church adhere to the Word of Wisdom was also undoubtedly given under inspiration. **There is, however, no known contemporary evidence of which I am aware that a separate new revelation changed the Word of Wisdom from a "principle with promise" to "a commandment" necessary for full participation in all the blessings of church membership.**

"One author on the subject has argued that the vote in 1880 sustaining the Doctrine and Covenants as binding on church membership was equivalent to a vote making the Word of Wisdom a commandment. If, however, the members were voting on the words contained in the book, what they did was to agree that the Word of Wisdom was "a principle with promise" not a commandment." 28

28 Roy W. Doxey, The Word of Wisdom Today (Salt Lake City: Deseret Book Company, 1975), pp. 13-14.

"… **It is much easier, therefore, to find references to previous statements than to see the presence of new, specific revelation.** The inclusion of coffee and tea and the exclusion of cocoa, for instance, from the prohibited substances can probably be attributed to statements of Joseph and Hyrum Smith and Brigham Young rather than to specific revelations."29

29 Some of the statements and reminiscences are cited in Doxey, pp. 10-13 and in John A. Widtsoe and Leah D. Widtsoe, The Word of Wisdom: A Modern Interpretation (Salt Lake City: Deseret Book Company, 1937), p. 28. **Here I am speaking of specific revelations rather than the type of revelation mentioned later in this article. I would differentiate between what might be termed instant and unexpected revelations and revelations derived from long and prayerful consideration of a particular problem under the inspiration of the Holy Spirit.**

Taken from THE WORD OF WISDOM: FROM PRINCIPLE TO REQUIREMENT THOMAS G. ALEXANDER

The current Handbook does not claim to be revelation or scripture (Handbook 0.0); therefore, its policies should not conflict with revelation, but such appears to be the case with the Word of Wisdom where the obedience-for-all policy is contrary to the only claimed revelation received – D&C 89 as revealed to the Prophet Joseph Smith as "not by commandment or constraint."

The Handbook's Introduction section (0.0) states:

> "The Lord taught, "Let every man learn his duty, and to act in the office in which he is appointed, in all diligence" (Doctrine and Covenants 107:99). As a leader in The Church of Jesus Christ of Latter-day Saints, you should seek personal revelation to help you learn and fulfill the duties of your calling.

> "Studying the scriptures and the teachings of latter-day prophets will help you understand and fulfill your duties. As you study the words of God, you will be more receptive to the influence of the Spirit (see Doctrine and Covenants 84:85).

> "You also learn your duties by studying the instructions in this handbook. These instructions can invite revelation if they are used to provide an understanding of principles, policies, and procedures to apply while seeking the guidance of the Spirit."

The administration of the Word of Wisdom is the responsibility of the current prophet who has the keys necessary to receive direct revelation from the Lord. While confusion at the highest levels of the Church is evident throughout this history, never-the-less this is the Lord's Church and while the facts can be embarrassing, the author has no intent to criticize Church leadership – they are accountable to the Lord, as we all are.

Until the Church addresses the Lord's meat proscription it falls short of the Lord's revealed "will." Also, until the Church explains "not by commandment or constraint, but … showing forth the order and will of God" (D&C 89:2) or provides a direct revelation from the Lord modifying the original revelation, it remains at odds with the Lord's word by making the Word of Wisdom a commandment for all members.

It is the author's desire that the Church grow in beauty and splendor by greater acceptance of the Lord's Word of Wisdom. It is time to restore the Lord's Word of Wisdom as it was revealed and follow it in the way the Prophet Joseph Smith required.

The kindness of the Lord in revealing to me a better understanding of the Word of Wisdom was done within my personal stewardship over my health. The Lord was honoring this stewardship and not violating President Nelson's. This was clearly stated in my *Report to President Nelson* in 2018. I believe that the Church will yet return to the Word of Wisdom administration practiced by the Prophet Joseph Smith. The period of sin was from not following the Joseph Smith administrative standard. The period of imposition came from the common practice of bureaucrats to constrain others to their views – not from revelation – else why so many changes? Was the Lord uncertain of His course? How could D&C 89:2 confound men who knew how to receive knowledge from God? If the Lord had not spoken to clarify it, why impose their own understanding?

I remember counseling with a Bishop who was selected more for his position in his culture than his ability to receive revelation. He was changing callings (under his stewardship) monthly – Young Men, Young Women, Sunday School, Primary, and Relief Society leaders and teachers. Members were becoming discouraged and some were leaving the Ward for another. I asked him how these callings could be inspired from the Lord? Was the Lord confused, unsure of Himself or those He called? God is not given to confusion. As Bishop he must give himself to much prayer and fasting and then receive revelation from God as to who should be called as the Presidents. He must then teach the presidents to seek and obtain revelation on who should be recommended for their councilors and teachers.

Additional revelation from the Lord on the Word of Wisdom has not been claimed or put forward for a sustaining vote of acceptance by the Church. The Lord's Priesthood Word of Wisdom Standard, practiced by the Prophet Joseph Smith, can be practiced today until the Lord has more to say on the topic.

CHAPTER SIX

APPLYING THE LORD'S PRIESTHOOD
WORD OF WISDOM STANDARD

The Prophet Joseph Smith, Jr.

I consider the December 2020 Word of Wisdom policy (Handbook 38.7.13) to be a partial restoration of the Lord's Priesthood Word of Wisdom standard as administered by the Prophet Joseph Smith. Under this restored policy, interpretation of the Lord's proscriptions is limited (except for Marijuana) to the Prophet Joseph Smith's understanding. This is not a complete restoration, but it is a significant improvement. This change should remove the many problems associated with the former policy that added multiple prohibitions without revelation from the Lord. This new policy confirms that additional revelation on the Word of Wisdom was not received – else why return to Joseph Smith's standard? The added prohibitions went well beyond the words of the Lord in D&C 89 and Joseph Smith's understanding. The Saints were not to use their own wisdom in avoiding other harmful and addictive substances. We will first look at how "Tobacco" and "hot drinks" were interpreted.

A. Tobacco and Vaping

A Stake President in Utah, one in Washington State, and one in North Carolina, all told me they had received no guidance from the Church on the question of electronic (e) cigarettes. This was prior to the Church prohibiting e-cigarettes, 15 Aug 2019 (https://newsroom. churchofjesuschrist.org/article/statement-word-of-wisdom-august-2019). One Stake President would not issue a Temple Recommend if one were an e-cigarette user based on the "appearance of evil" and two did not know how they would rule.

Many who conquered smoking Tobacco by using e-cigarettes considered that they were in obedience to the Word of Wisdom and should have been issued Temple Recommends. They were not using Tobacco – just nicotine, the chemical in Tobacco that increases alertness but is addictive. However, the sweeping pre-Dec-2020-Handbook statement against "harmful or habit-forming substances except under the care of a competent physician" clearly proscribed self-medication with e-cigarettes as did the 15 August 2019 Official Church Statement on the Word of Wisdom.

As missionaries in the Addiction Recovery Program, we served an elderly man who had stopped smoking (Tobacco) as required by his priesthood leaders. He achieved that by using e-cigarettes. It was deeply discouraging to him that he was then asked to also stop e-cigarettes before receiving a Temple Recommend. Under this restored standard he should be approved if worthy in all other areas.

The December 2020 policy does not include additional restrictions (except for marijuana) and the one reference to "vaping" (the current term for using e-cigarettes) is found in the medical marijuana policy (Handbook 38.7.9) which allows for vaping marijuana if medically approved "based on medical necessity." Since the Handbook is used to consolidate Church policies the referenced Church policy prohibiting "vaping or e-cigarettes, green tea, and coffee-based products" has also been dropped by the new policy's adherence to Joseph Smith's understanding of the revelation he received from the Lord (D&C 89). The policy is once again "abstinence from tobacco, strong drinks (alcohol), and hot drinks (tea and coffee)." All other substance use (except for Marijuana) that may be harmful, illegal, etc. is for the member to "avoid" and therefore does not come under Word of Wisdom prohibition. Thus, vaping becomes something members are encouraged to "avoid" but would not restrict them from a Temple Recommend. Illegal drug use should still be restrictive under the commandment to obey the law of the land.

B. Hot Drinks – Tea and Coffee

The 15 August 2019 Church policy identifying green tea (Camellia sinensis) as restricted under the Word of Wisdom is correct. Many members have thought that the Prophet Joseph Smith was referring to black (English) tea and that green tea with its excellent properties as an herb was not included. However, black tea is green tea that has been dried to concentrate and preserve its flavor.
See https://www.teamuse.com/article_031001.html

The English teas drunk prior to the American revolution were heavily oxidized black tea mixtures but these were not prevalent in the early 1800's when the Word of Wisdom was received. Post revolution, the teas consumed in the United States were imported by American merchants directly from China. They were usually Bohea, Hyson and Congou teas – all described as green teas often dried to preserve their flavor with a resulting dark or black appearance.

Tea was extremely popular but also expensive, so "In consequence of evils and designs which (did) … exist in the hearts of conspiring men in (Joseph Smith's) … days, (the Lord gave us) this word of wisdom by revelation (D&C 89:4)." Tea was so commonly adulterated the British Parliament past several acts against it. Sloe-leaf and other not harmful things were common, but so also were harmful things such as dyes for color and sheep dung!

A 1785 publication by Richard Twining, **Observations on the Tea and Window Act, And On The Tea Trade**, included these recipes for adulterated or "Smouch" tea:

> " *Method of making* Smouch *with Aſh Tree leaves, to mix with Black Teas.*
>
> " When gathered they are firſt dried in the ſun, then baked, they are next put upon a floor and trod upon until the leaves are ſmall, then ſifted and ſteeped in copperas, with ſheeps dung ; after which being dried on a floor, they are fit for uſe."
>
> *Another Mode.*
>
> " When the leaves are gathered they are boiled in a copper with copperas and ſheeps dung ; when the liquor is ſtrained off, they are baked and trod upon, until the leaves are ſmall, after which they are fit for uſe.

The recipes read (emphasis is the author's):

> "Method of making Smouch with Ash Tree Leaves to mix with Black Teas. When gathered they are first dried in the sun then baked. They are next put on the floor and trod upon until the leaves are small, then lifted and steeped in copperas, with **sheep's dung**, after which, being dried on the floor, they are fit for use.
>
> "Another Mode.
>
> "When the leaves are gathered they are boiled in a copper with copperas and **sheeps dung**; when the liquor is strained off, they are baked and trod upon, until the leaves are small, after which they are fit for use."

The adulteration of tea also occurred in China – the prime supplier. It wasn't until the late 1800's that regulations put an end to the problem of smouch tea, so the Word of Wisdom was very sound wisdom indeed in 1833.

Coffee was also adulterated using inexpensive Chicory root which also served as a much healthier substitute for coffee, was caffeine free, and is still available today.
See https://www.healthline.com/nutrition/chicory-coffee

It may be that the Lord had tea in mind because of its adulteration and coffee for its high levels of caffeine (~95 mg per cup – three times that of tea) but the Lord's specific words were "hot drinks", and we can all be cautious of very hot drinks of any kind including soups. In the Word of Wisdom, we also see the Lord's preference for "all wholesome herbs (which) God hath ordained for the constitution, nature, and use of man—Every herb in the season thereof, … to be used with prudence and thanksgiving (D&C 89:10-11)." We also read His preference for "mild drinks (D&C 89:17)" (as opposed to "hot drinks") which are a healthy way to use wholesome herbs and grains.

What do we consider hot versus mild? I gained a better understanding through two experiences:

As a youth in New Zealand, I was invited to have a cup of tea with a friend at his home. I requested and received hot chocolate. Both drinks were prepared with boiling water from the kettle. Before I could touch the very hot chocolate my friend had finished his tea.

As an adult in Japan, I enjoyed ramen soups with my family. At a ramen stand in Osaka we witnessed a man complete his bowl of ramen before we could touch ours.

My definition of hot changed – I was enjoying warm/mild chocolate and ramen. Joseph Smith's clarification of tea and coffee does not permit us to drink other scalding drinks and soups. Likewise, in my view, Joseph's reference to coffee and tea does not restrict us from mild or iced tea and coffee – although I choose to not drink them at all. However, I do use an anti-cancer supplement that includes the compounds in tea that have been identified as anti-cancer.

Herbal drinks are used in cultures around the world for health. Each culture has their favorites. This list of "seven wonder leaves" used for herb teas in the Philippines was provided by Vivian Burr who I was privileged to teach and baptize when I was serving as a missionary in Manila. Your culture will have similar lists.

- Banaba (Lagerstroemia speciosa)
- Alagaw (Premna odorata)
- Cainito (Chrysophyllum cainito)
- Pandan (Pandanus amaryllifolius)
- Guava (Psidium guajava)
- Star Anise (Illicium verum)
- Cilantro (Coriandrum sativum)

Based on the Word of Wisdom revelation and the new Church policy, members can drink "mild drinks" brewed from these "herbs" with the guidance to "<u>avoid</u> substances that are harmful, illegal, or addictive or that impair judgment … (and) to <u>use wisdom and prayerful judgment</u> in making choices to promote (your) physical, spiritual, and emotional health."

C. Commandment or Not?

As we approach 200 years from the time of the Word of Wisdom revelation, Church leaders are still not following the Lord's words in the Word of Wisdom, and the Priesthood and leadership standard established by the Prophet Joseph Smith in 1834. The Church has changed the Word of Wisdom into a commandment for all members and expect them to live a standard that ignores the Lord's proscriptions on meat, and prior to Dec 2020, expanded the proscriptions to hundreds of substances – all without any reported revelation from the Lord.

Is it appropriate for us to change the Lord's meaning from "not by commandment or constraint" to commandment and constraint for everyone, when He has provided His own transition through the Oath and Covenant of the Priesthood? When we consider that the Word of Wisdom is a "commandment" only for those entering the Oath and Covenant of the Priesthood, then we can understand that it is not "by commandment or constraint" for those entering the Church through baptism. The early Church did not make obedience to the Word of Wisdom a requirement for baptism. It was required for ordination to the Melchizedek Priesthood and any leadership position in the Church.

D. Suggested Recommend Questions

The following discussion and recommend questions for baptism and a Temple Recommend is for consideration. I put this forward with the title, *The Lord's Priesthood Word of Wisdom Standard,* **to distinguish it from the current practice. I include the personal revelation I received as if it were confirmed by the Lord to the Prophet. <u>I realize this decision is not mine to make for the Church, but the Lord's through His appointed Prophet.</u>**

This recommendation does not address Marijuana. Refer to the Church Handbook 38.7.9 quoted in Chapter 5, Page 67.

We can accept the word of the Lord in D&C 89 as correct and fully apply the Word of Wisdom as He intended by understanding that:

1. *"Anything that doth enslave the soul of man is not of God, but of him that desireth that all men might be miserable like unto himself."* However, the only proscriptions in the Word of Wisdom are: no tobacco, no alcohol, no hot drinks (tea and coffee), and the flesh of beasts and fowl be eaten sparingly.
2. The Word of Wisdom is "not (a) commandment or constraint." It is not a requirement for baptism and the remission of sins. It does not keep one from the Church or the Celestial Kingdom – just exaltation within the Celestial Kingdom.
3. The Word of Wisdom is "the <u>order</u> and will of God" for all of us to follow by choice as a "principle with promise."
4. Those who are under the Oath and Covenant of the Priesthood ["the holiest <u>order</u> of God"] are commanded "to live by every word that proceedeth forth from the mouth of God" – this includes obedience to the Word of Wisdom for those:
   a. Receiving the priesthood.
   b. Receiving Temple ordinances given under the Oath and Covenant of the Priesthood.

The Lord's Priesthood Word of Wisdom Standard is based on the Lord's language in the revelation (D&C 89), the Oath and Covenant of the Priesthood (D&C 84: 33-48), the decision of the Prophet Joseph Smith and the Kirtland and Missouri High Councils in 1834, and the Handbook. The personal revelation I received is included as a correct principle but can only be used for the Church with the Lord's word to the Prophet.

It appears that there is great opportunity to recover far more of the children of God through a graduated program of:

1. Faith in Christ first for an unbaptized associate member of the Church caught up in sin
2. Repentance from sin (not Word of Wisdom violation) and baptism for membership in the Church and the Gift of the Holy Ghost
3. Obedience to the Word of Wisdom for Priesthood ordination and Temple covenants

Suggested Priesthood Word of Wisdom Standard (D&C 89; 84: 18, 33-48) **Interview Questions:**
*In this standard, the Word of Wisdom includes proscribed items listed in D&C 89 **only** as now also in the Dec 2020 Handbook. "Anything that doth enslave the soul of man is not of God, but of him that desireth that all men might be miserable like unto himself" is a new understanding but includes no proscriptions. Obedience to the Word of Wisdom is not required for membership but is for Priesthood ordination and the making of Temple covenants. For those suffering from legal addictions, attending the Addiction Recovery Program under the care of a Bishop is recommended. Those suffering under illegal addictions could be received as unbaptized associate members and be invited to prepare for baptism through the Addiction Recovery Program.*

1. Word of Wisdom obedience not be required for baptism and confirmation
    a. Word of Wisdom questions for baptism [Answer required for baptism]:
        i. Have you read the Word of Wisdom revelation (D&C 89)? [Yes]
        ii. Do you accept that to be ordained to the Priesthood, make Temple covenants, or hold a leadership position in the Church, that you must obey the Word of Wisdom? [Yes]
        iii. Do you understand the Lord's Word of Wisdom standard includes not using Tobacco, alcoholic drinks, the hot drinks tea and coffee, and to eat "flesh … of beasts and … fowls … sparingly"? [Yes]

iv. Do you "use any substance that contains <u>illegal</u> drugs?" [No]
If "Yes"
   a) Are you under medical care for your addiction?
   OR
   b) Are you attending an addiction recovery program?
      If "No"
      1) Will you attend the Addiction Recovery Program of the Church?

Persons using an <u>illegal</u> substance would **not** be baptism candidates. Such persons could be accepted as unbaptized associate members and prepare for baptism if they are under medical care **or** are, or will, commit to attending the Addiction Recovery Program of the Church.

b. Persons who have an addiction can be greatly benefited from Church membership. New associate or regular members with Word of Wisdom issues can be encouraged to access the power of the Atonement of Jesus Christ to overcome their addictions by:
   i. Receiving a Priesthood blessing
   ii. Seeking the Spirit by applying themselves to the Gift of the Holy Ghost
   iii. Daily prayer and Book of Mormon study.

   President Russell M. Nelson:
   "I promise that as you daily immerse yourself in the Book of Mormon, you can be immunized against the evils of the day, even the gripping plague of pornography and other mind-numbing addictions."

   iv. Attendance at an addiction recovery program. The Church Addiction Recovery Program would be recommended and is an excellent meeting for investigators

v. Members with Word of Wisdom issues would govern themselves on when to take the Sacrament. The Lord is generous in providing the Sacrament weekly. This is particularly important to those suffering from addiction, since recovery from addiction is typically a slow process with relapses, and the weekly opportunity to renew one's covenants with the Lord is empowering. Members can be encouraged to prepare themselves for the Sacrament each week by having faith in Christ and repenting of their sins. They can be taught that the condition of addiction is not a sin, but sins committed in addiction need to be repented of (e.g. physical and virtual sex outside of marriage, theft, etc.).

2. Word of Wisdom obedience not be required for ordination to Aaronic Priesthood offices; however, Bishops should see movement on the part of the candidate to become obedient.
3. Word of Wisdom obedience not be required for a Limited Use Temple Recommend; however, Bishops should see significant progress on the part of the candidate to becoming obedient. Members would be encouraged to participate in Temple baptisms and confirmations for the dead. They would also be encouraged to do this work for their own dead.
4. Obedience to the Word of Wisdom be required for:
    a. Aaronic Priesthood and Young Women leadership positions
    b. Teacher positions
    c. Ordination to Elder
    d. Ward presidency positions, Bishopric, Stake or higher callings
    e. A full Temple Recommend

5. The full Temple Recommend Word of Wisdom questions
    [Answer for a recommend]:
    a. Do you understand and keep the Word of Wisdom as
        outlined in D&C 89? [Yes]
    b. Do you keep *The Lord's Priesthood Word of Wisdom
        Standard* which includes not using Tobacco,
        alcoholic drinks, the hot drinks tea and coffee, and to
        eat "flesh … of beasts and … fowls … sparingly"?
        [Yes]
        i. Do you "use any substance that contains
            <u>illegal</u> drugs?" [No]
            If "Yes"
                a) Are you under medical care for your
                    addiction?
                OR
                b) Are you attending the Addiction
                    Recovery Program of the Church
                    under the care of your Bishop?
        As shown here, persons using an illegal substance
        would not receive a Temple Recommend and would
        be encouraged to enter medical care **or** attend the
        Addiction Recovery Program of the Church under the
        care of their Bishop.

Benefits of this Standard:
1. The personal revelation that *"Anything that doth enslave the
    soul of man is not of God, but of him that desireth that all
    men might be miserable like unto himself"* can only be added
    to the Word of Wisdom under the Lord's direction to the
    Prophet. In the context of this work it is part of *The Lord's
    Priesthood Word of Wisdom Standard* provided for Church
    consideration and to help individuals meet the "will of God in
    the[ir] temporal salvation."
2. The Lord has not declared the Word of Wisdom a
    commandment or sin for which repentance is required for
    baptism. A "principle with promise … (for) … temporal
    salvation" is not restricting a person from a spiritual and
    eternal salvation.

3. *The Lord's Priesthood Word of Wisdom Standard* (D&C 89; 84: 18, 33-48), adopted by the Prophet Joseph Smith and the Kirtland High Council, is not applied to all members – it is applied to leaders and those covenanting under the Oath and Covenant of the Priesthood.
4. The proscription of eating meat other than sparingly is included in the standard.
5. Candidates will judge themselves with a much clearer understanding of Word of Wisdom proscriptions.
6. Additional proscriptions are not added to the Word of Wisdom without direct revelation.
7. Clearer standards prevent proscriptions developing that vary depending on differing views of Mission Presidents, Bishops and Stake Presidents.
8. These questions will help stop the "cultural Mormonisms" that have developed around the Word of Wisdom. The tendency for members to judge others on appearances is not good, "for the Lord seeth not as man seeth; for man looketh on the outward appearance, but the Lord looketh on the heart." (1 Sam 16:7)
9. Any addicted person who has faith in Christ will benefit from the blessings of the Lord's Church and the Atonement of Jesus Christ through:
    a. Unbaptized Associate Member status for those using illegal drugs while being "nourished by the good word of God" through the Addiction Recovery Program of the Church as they prepare for baptism.
    b. Regular member status for those addicted to proscribed Word of Wisdom substances while being "nourished by the good word of God" through the Addiction Recovery Program of the Church as they prepare for Priesthood ordination and the Temple.

CONCLUSION

Within my health stewardship, The Lord revealed Word of Wisdom principles which require my obedience and suggest the Prophet fully restore the Priesthood standard applied by Joseph Smith:

1. As I prepared to take the Sacrament in May 2018, the Lord gave me a clear understanding of the "principle" underlying the Word of Wisdom. He said:

   "Anything that doth enslave the soul of man is not of God, but of him that desireth that all men might be miserable like unto himself."

2. The Lord then showed me that His administrative guideline for the Word of Wisdom (D&C 89: 1-3) is precise and not confusing. It is not appropriate or necessary for us to change the Lord's words from "not by commandment" to commandment for all. The Lord has His own transition to obedience within this guideline. I call this *The Lord's Priesthood Word of Wisdom Standard*.
   a. The covenants of baptism include one to "keep His commandments" (Mosiah 18: 8-10) and the Lord declared the Word of Wisdom to be "<u>not by commandment or constraint</u>." It is not a commandment that must be repented of to qualify for baptism. Taking the proscribed substances into our bodies harms ourselves, not others. Repentance is required for sins against others, whether under the influence of proscribed substances or not. Addiction by itself is not a sin.
   b. His word also "(shows) forth the <u>order</u> and will of God" which has two meanings:
      i. For "all Saints" it refers to the natural <u>order</u> that God has established. "All Saints" benefit from following the "<u>order</u> and will of God" for their "temporal salvation."
      ii. It also refers to "the holiest <u>order</u> of God" (D&C 84: 18) entered through Priesthood ordination or Temple ordinances. By baptism we qualify for the Celestial Kingdom without a commandment to obey the Word of Wisdom, but by Priesthood ordination and obedience to "every word (of wisdom) … from … God" (D&C 84: 43-44 [33-48]) we are exalted.

Church history shows a period of **Obedience (1833-1844)** as the Prophet Joseph Smith understood and applied these principles. In 1834, he established and enforced obedience to the Word of Wisdom for ordination to the Priesthood and leadership positions in the Church. This enforcement is illustrated by the release of the Missouri Presidency in 1838. In 1840, he vigorously opposed strict "abstinence" for all members as "pharisaical and hypocritical." The higher standard for the Priesthood remained, tempered by self-medicated use of alcohol, tea, and coffee which was acceptable "when needed." In 1843, Twenty-two men were ordained Elders "with this express injunction, that they quit the use of tobacco and keep the Word of Wisdom." **(See APPENDIX: 1833-1843)**

A long period of **Sin (1844-1921)** followed the Prophet Joseph's martyrdom. *The Lord's Priesthood Word of Wisdom Standard* was not strictly observed, and leaders began again to advocate for abstinence by all members, even while leaders were NOT in obedience. For example, by public admission, in October 1862 Conference, President Brigham Young did not stop chewing tobacco, and drinking tea and coffee, until 1860, nine years after an 1851 Conference "covenant to leave off … all things mentioned in the Word of Wisdom." In 1869 he said, "Very well, (it is not a commandment) but we are commanded to observe every word that proceeds from the mouth of God," seeking again to apply the Priesthood standard to all Saints. **(See APPENDIX: 1844-1921)**

Since 1921 we have been in a season of **Imposition (1921-Present)** rather than "greeting … revelation and … wisdom." Leaders who say the Word of Wisdom is a commandment are correct – they are under the "Oath and Covenant of the Priesthood," but investigators and some members are not. In 1921, President Heber J. Grant required obedience for a Temple Recommend and in 1930 for missionaries, thus partially restoring *The Lord's Priesthood Word of Wisdom Standard*, but then applied it to investigators and all members. No clarifying revelation has been claimed or published. The Lord can redirect by revelation, as He did with Peter to preach the gospel to the gentiles, and Wilford Woodruff to end polygamy. However, Word of Wisdom scripture remains "not by commandment or constraint."

By the same "pharisaical" action the Prophet Joseph rejected, the pre-Dec-2020-Handbooks' proscription of "harmful or habit-forming substances except under the care of a competent physician" expected investigators and all members to live a standard that significantly expanded proscriptions without any reported revelation. These were subject to the personal interpretation of Priesthood interviewers and many with addictions were barred from baptism and the Temple. Addicted people often commit sin, but the condition of addiction is not sin. Changing the word of God is certainly sin, even if prompted by a lack of understanding, or a zeal to improve the lot of all men.

It is time to fully live the Word of Wisdom given by the Lord "not by commandment or constraint, but … showing forth the order and will of God" and as correctly applied by the Prophet Joseph Smith.

The Lord's Priesthood Word of Wisdom Standard could restore the Church to the full blessings of the Lord's Word of Wisdom in that:
1. The only proscriptions are those in the Word of Wisdom.
2. The "flesh also of beasts and … fowls … to be used sparingly" is included.
3. **ALL are encouraged to follow the will of God by living the Word of Wisdom.**
4. The Lord provides baptism for those who come unto Him in faith, repenting of their disobedience to His commandments. The Word of Wisdom is "not by commandment or constraint." Therefore:
   a. Those who have faith in Christ but are addicted to illegal substances could be received as unbaptized associate members while they prepare for baptism "nourished by the good word of God" in the Addiction Recovery Program of the Church.
   b. Those addicted to legal substances could be baptized and attend the Addiction Recovery Program as they prepare for ordination to the Priesthood and Temple ordinances.

Following the Prophet Joseph Smith's death, Church leaders fell into sin under the Prophet Brigham Young. Without revelation from the Lord he and succeeding prophets changed the Word of Wisdom into a commandment and began to enforce standards the Prophet Joseph described as "pharisaical and hypocritical."

Specifically, they struggled to implement the "will of God in the temporal salvation of <u>all saints</u>" with great diligence, while failing to get the leadership corps to comply with the Prophet Joseph's leadership standard and neglected the meat proscription.

There has been no direct word from God changing the Word of Wisdom into a "commandment" and requiring it for baptism, or that has expanded our understanding by providing additional "forewarn(ings)."

The Oath and Covenant of the Priesthood (D&C 84: 43-44 [33-48]) clearly brings the Word of Wisdom under commandment for those in the Covenant. However, from at least 2010 to the pre-Dec-2020-Handbook the Church added a myriad of proscriptions on all members without any apparent direct revelation from the Lord while it failed to emphasize the Lord's meat proscription. The convert candidate for baptism is asked, "Are you willing to obey … The Word of Wisdom?" and the candidate for a Temple Recommend is asked "Do you understand and obey the Word of Wisdom?" It was highly likely that most members and leaders did not, given the Church's proscription prior to December 2020 of "any harmful or habit-forming substances except under the care of a competent physician," and the on-going un-emphasized meat proscription of the Lord.

The December 2020 Handbook has significantly changed Church policy in a very positive and simplified way. President Russell M. Nelson's update to the Word of Wisdom in December 2020 removes the additional restrictions that could only be used "under the care of a competent physician" completely, except for Marijuana.

The Handbook now states:

> 38.7.13.

> "… Prophets have clarified that the teachings in Doctrine and Covenants 89 include <u>abstinence from</u> tobacco, strong drinks (alcohol), and hot drinks (tea and coffee).

> "Prophets have also taught members to <u>avoid</u> substances that are harmful, illegal, or addictive or that impair judgment.

"There are other harmful substances and practices that are not specified in the Word of Wisdom or by Church leaders. Members should <u>use wisdom and prayerful judgment</u> in making choices to promote their physical, spiritual, and emotional health."

… and for marijuana:

38.7.9

"<u>The Church opposes the use of marijuana for non-medical purposes</u>.

"… The Church does not approve of vaping marijuana unless the medical provider has authorized it based on medical necessity.

"The Church does not approve of smoking marijuana, including for medical purposes."

The Church still insists that "The Word of Wisdom is a commandment of God" (Handbook 38.7.13) while the only claimed revelation from the Lord states it is "not by commandment or constraint" (D&C 89: 2) and Church claims that it became a commandment in 1851 under President Brigham Young are not supported by the historic record.

The Word of Wisdom certainly has been a commandment for all of those who have taken upon themselves the Oath and Covenant of the Priesthood, but not for converts and members who have not yet entered that Covenant.

The Lord's "not(s)" are restored by President Nelson's December 2020 policy. All that we need now is for the leaders of the Church to gain an understanding of the Lord's phrase describing the Word of Wisdom as given "not by commandment or constraint, but … showing forth the <u>order</u> and will of God" as was applied by the Prophet Joseph Smith and described in this work.

I have every confidence in what the Lord taught me within my stewardship about the Word of Wisdom. That knowledge, along with this December 2020 partial restoration, gives me every confidence that the truth about the Word of Wisdom will once again be fully restored and understood to the benefit of God's children and their greater access to the grace of His Son.

"Say nothing but repentance unto this generation" (D&C 11: 9) seems germane to leaders and regular members of the Church with respect to our acceptance of the Word of Wisdom today; for "all saints who remember to keep and do these sayings, walking in obedience to the commandments, shall receive health in their navel and marrow to their bones; and shall find wisdom and great treasures of knowledge, even hidden treasures; and shall run and not be weary, and shall walk and not faint. And I, the Lord, give unto them a promise, that the destroying angel shall pass by them, as the children of Israel, and not slay them. Amen." (D&C 89: 18-21)

APPENDIX

<u>A TIMELINE OF WORD OF WISDOM COMPLIANCE</u>

It is evident from all public sources I have accessed, that the Lord has not spoken more concerning the Word of Wisdom to anyone in the leadership of the Church since the original revelation, 27 Feb 1833. No prophet since Joseph Smith has claimed direct revelation from the Lord modifying D&C 89 in any way. Two years after the Oath and Covenant of the Priesthood (D&C 84) was received, and one year after the Word of Wisdom (D&C 89) was received, Joseph Smith and the Kirtland High Council officially accepted the Word of Wisdom as a standard for those "hold(ing) an office" in the Church to "obey." Records show that obedience was enforced in the release of the Missouri Presidency in 1838, and for the ordination of 22 Elders as late as 1843. Joseph also vigorously opposed an "abstinence" standard for all Saints in 1840. However, since Joseph's martyrdom, leaders of the Church did not enforce the ordination/leadership standard and generally encouraged <u>all</u> members to obey the "will of God" while leaders were falling short.

The current claim that the Word of Wisdom became a commandment at a September 1851, Conference is not supported by the records. The Conference attendees (except for men older than 90) "covenant(ed) to leave off the use of tobacco, whisky, and all things mentioned in the Word of Wisdom." By his own report, Brigham Young did not "leave off" chewing tobacco, tea, and coffee, until 1860. In 1869, Brigham Young did argue that it was a "commandment" for all members even though he referenced no new revelation but referred to a scripture that applied only to those under the Oath and Covenant of the Priesthood. Following his own repentance, Brigham Young required obedience to the Word of Wisdom for a recommend to attend the Saint George Temple.

Despite the action of Joseph Smith and the Kirtland High Council, and the 1851 vote, the Word of Wisdom was not strictly obeyed by Church leaders until 1921 when it was again made a requirement for a Temple Recommend by President Heber J. Grant. In 1930 he also required that new missionaries not use tobacco. About this same time, the Word of Wisdom became a requirement for baptism, and therefore all members – not just leaders. However, the Word of Wisdom "sent (by) greeting; not by commandment or constraint ..." remains unchanged by any claimed revelation from the Lord.

1833 – 1844	Obedience	98
1844 - 1921	Sin	101
1921 - Present	Imposition	116

<u>**OBEDIENCE**</u>**: 1833-1844**

1833 – Feb: The Word of Wisdom is received by Revelation to the Prophet Joseph Smith:

D&C 89: 1 **<u>A Word of Wisdom</u>**, for the benefit of the council of high priests, assembled in Kirtland, and the church, and also the saints in Zion—
2 To be sent greeting; **<u>not by commandment or constraint</u>, but by revelation and the word of wisdom, showing forth the order and <u>will of God in the temporal salvation of all saints</u> in the last days—**
3 Given for **<u>a principle with promise</u>**, adapted to the capacity of the weak and the weakest of all saints, who are or can be called saints. (*See Page 8 for the full quote.*)

1834 – Feb: The Church declares members worthy to hold office if they obey the Word of Wisdom:

In February 1834, the High Council of the Church, over which the Presidency of the Church presided, asked:
"Whether disobedience to the word of wisdom was a transgression sufficient to deprive an official member from holding office in the Church, after having it sufficiently taught him?" After a free and full discussion, Joseph Smith the Prophet gave the following decision which was unanimously accepted by the council: "No official member in this Church is worthy to hold an office after having the word of wisdom properly taught him; and he, the official member, neglecting to comply with and obey it."
Teachings of the Prophet Joseph Smith, Joseph Fielding Smith, p. 117

Minutes, 20 Feb. 1834. A meeting of the Missouri high council and others passed a similar resolution sometime later, stating that they would "not fellowship any ordained member who will or does not observe the word of Wisdom according to its litteral [sic] reading."
Minute Book 2, p. 71.

1837 – May: Confirming the leadership standard:

"Have not the authorities of the church in council assembled in this place, decided deliberately and positively," wrote a Church editorialist at Kirtland in 1837, "that if any official members of this church shall violate or in any wise disregard the words of wisdom which the Lord has given for the benefit of his saints, he shall lose his office?"
> W. A. Cowdery, Messenger and Advocate, May 1837, 510. From: Paul H. Peterson and Ronald W. Walker, "Brigham Young's Word of Wisdom Legacy," BYU Studies, vol. 42, nos. 3–4 (2003), 29–64.

1838 – February: The Missouri Presidency turned "out of their presidential office" for Word of Wisdom infractions and "for selling their lands in Jackson County."
Enforcement of the 1834 standard is evidenced by the 1838 case against the Missouri Presidency, David Whitmer, William Phelps, John Whitmer, and Oliver Cowdery.

"At a February (1838) council meeting, George Morey, a high councilor, set "forth in a very energetic manner, the proceedings of the Presidency as being iniquitous." **The four were accused of various infractions of the Word of Wisdom** and of selling their lands in Jackson County, signaling a lack of faith in the Saints' return to their promised land. **Cowdery admitted to drinking tea three times a day for his health, and the Whitmers contended tea and coffee were not covered by the revelation.** As for their property, the four threatened to leave if they were forbidden to sell their Jackson lands. Phelps said he "would move out of the accursed place." Moreover, they "would not be controlled by an ecclesiastical power of revelation whatever in their temporal concerns."
"Considering the answers unsatisfactory, **the council removed the four from office.**"
> Taken from *Joseph Smith, Rough Stone Rolling* by Richard Lyman Bushman, 346-347.

1838 – April: President Joseph Smith, said in conference, the Word of Wisdom "should be observed."

> "On 7 April 1838, President Joseph Smith, Jr., said in conference, the Word of Wisdom "should be observed.""
> *Teachings of the Prophet Joseph Smith*, Joseph Fielding Smith, p. 117

1840 – President Joseph Smith does not support abstinence for all members:

> "… in Nauvoo, Joseph Smith declined to enforce a policy of abstinence. After one Church elder preached a long sermon that enjoined the Saints to "sanctity, solemnity, and temperance in the extreme, in the rigid sectarian style," Joseph reproved him for being "pharisaical and hypocritical and [for] not edifying the people." Later that evening, a Church council concluded "that a forced abstinence was not making us free but we should be under bondage with a yoak [sic] upon our necks."[17]
>
> > 17 Joseph Smith Jr., History of The Church of Jesus Christ of Latter-day Saints, ed. B. H. Roberts, 2d. ed., rev., 7 vols. (Salt Lake City: Deseret Book, 1971), 4:445; Wilford Woodruff, Wilford Woodruff's Journal: 1833–1898, Typescript, ed. Scott G. Kenny, 9 vols. (Midvale, Utah: Signature Books, 1983–1984), 2:136–37, November 7, 1841.
> > Taken from Paul H. Peterson and Ronald W. Walker, "Brigham Young's Word of Wisdom Legacy," BYU Studies, vol. 42, nos. 3–4 (2003), 29–64.

1843 – April: President Joseph Smith requires Word of Wisdom obedience for ordination to Elder.

> Twenty-two men were ordained "with this express injunction, that they quit the use of tobacco and keep the Word of Wisdom."
> Historian's Office, JS History, Draft Notes, 10 Apr. 1843.

Author's Comment:
Following the death of the Prophet Joseph, it appears that the leadership standard was not enforced up until President Heber J. Grant required obedience to the Word of Wisdom for a Temple Recommend, and that those Elders called on missions not be smokers. There are numerous references to leaders in the highest councils of the Church not strictly following the Word of Wisdom. By his own record, President Brigham Young did not live it until 1860. As President of the Twelve Apostles, I assume he must have been obedient during Joseph's life.

1847 – March: Brigham Young admits to chewing tobacco:

> "In March 1847, as the pioneer camp was about to go west, he spoke about making the Word of Wisdom a test of fellowship. While sickness might bring the use of a "cup of tea or a little sp[irits]," Brigham urged that the Saints generally put aside their whiskey and tobacco. They would see, he said, "who is King, tobacco or the man." There was a measure of self-inspection in his statement. "If I was not afflicted with chewing [tobacco]," he told the Saints, "I should be just right" with the Word of Wisdom." [22]
>
> 22 General Church Minutes, March 21 and 26, 1847. From Paul H. Peterson and Ronald W. Walker, "Brigham Young's Word of Wisdom Legacy," BYU Studies, vol. 42, nos. 3–4 (2003), 29–64.

1851 – Sept 9: President Brigham Young calls for a covenant to keep the Word of Wisdom:

In *Answers to Gospel Questions, 1: 197,* Joseph Fielding Smith answers the following question:
> "Will you please tell me if the Word of Wisdom has ever been presented to the Church as a commandment making its observation obligatory upon the members of the Church?"

He answers:
> "The simple answer to this question is yes, such commandment has been given and repeated on several occasions.

"September 9, 1851, President Brigham Young stated that
the members of the Church had had sufficient time to be
taught the import of this revelation and that henceforth it was
to be considered a divine commandment. This was first put
to vote before the female members of the congregation and
then before the men and by unanimous vote accepted.
President Joseph F. Smith at a conference meeting in
October 1908, made the same statement, and this has been
repeated from time to time."

The 1851 Conference action by Brigham Young to place the women
and then the men (under 90) under covenant to keep all the
prohibitions of the Word of Wisdom is often cited as him declaring it
to be a commandment for all members of the Church, not just
leaders, yet we do not find the word "commandment" anywhere in
the **"Minutes of the General Conference"**.

"The Patriarch [**John Smith**] again rose to speak on the
Word of Wisdom, and urging on the brethren to leave off
using tobacco, &c.

"President Young rose to put the motion and called on all the
sisters who will leave off the use of tea, coffee, &c., to
manifest it by raising the right hand; seconded and carried.

And then put the following motion; calling on all the boys
[*sic*] who were under ninety years of age who would
**covenant to leave off the use of tobacco, whisky, and <u>all</u>
<u>things mentioned</u> in the Word of Wisdom,** to manifest it in
the same manner, which was carried unanimously."

"The Patriarch then said, may the Lord bless you and help
you to keep all your covenants. Amen.

"President Young amongst other things said he knew the
goodness of the people, and the Lord bears with our
weakness; we must serve the Lord, and those who go with
me will keep the Word of Wisdom, and if the High Priests,
the Seventies, the Elders, and others will not serve the Lord,
we will sever them from the Church. I will draw the line, and
know who is for the Lord and who is not, and those who will
not keep the Word of Wisdom, I will cut off from the Church; I
throw out a challenge to all men and women."[32]

"Minutes of the General Conference", Tuesday, Sep. 9, 1851, afternoon session; *Millennial Star*, 1 February 1852, vol. 14, p. 35. Taken from Wikipedia: Word of Wisdom https://en.wikipedia.org/wiki/Word_of_Wisdom#Emphasized_by_Brigham_Young

From Paul H. Peterson and Ronald W. Walker, "Brigham Young's Word of Wisdom Legacy," BYU Studies, vol. 42, nos. 3–4 (2003), 29–64:

> **"The September 1851 Conference in Review.** Church leaders would later refer to the September 1851 conference as the point in time when Joseph Smith's revelation was accepted by the members of the Church as a binding commandment." 46

> 46 For instance, see Francis M. Lyman, in Seventy-Ninth Annual Conference of The Church of Jesus Christ of Latter-day Saints (Salt Lake City: The Church of Jesus Christ of Latter-day Saints, 1908), 55; and McCue, "Did the Word of Wisdom Become a Commandment in 1851?" 66–77.
>
> See Joseph Fielding Smith, Improvement Era 59 (February 1956): 78. This influential article responded to this question: Has the Word of Wisdom "ever been presented to the Church as a commandment making its observance obligatory upon the members of the Church?" To this inquiry, Elder Smith replied, "The simple answer to this question is yes, such commandment has been given and repeated on several occasions. [On] September 9, 1851, President Brigham Young stated that the members of the Church had had sufficient time to be taught the import of this revelation and that henceforth it was to be considered a divine commandment." Elder Smith's statement was later quoted in various books, Church Sunday School manuals, and seminary and institute manuals. The most recent reference to the supposedly pivotal 1851 conference action was made by President Ezra Taft Benson in his address to the April 1983 general conference. Ezra Taft Benson, "A Principle with a Promise," Ensign 13 (May 1983): 53.

"However, little evidence exists that Brigham himself regarded this September conference as a pivotal event in Word of Wisdom reform. Certainly, he took no steps, then or later, to make full compliance a membership test for either Church leaders or the members in general." [47]

> 47 When the city's bishops met at their regular coordinating meeting in October 1851, there was telling uncertainty about the recent Word of Wisdom counsel. Had the recent conference made the health code "a Law in Israel?" asked one of the bishops. Presiding Bishop Edward Hunter ended the meeting's discussion by saying that "as for making . . . [the Word of Wisdom] a Test of fellowship he could not at present decide."
>> Record of Bishops' Meetings, October 12, 1851, "Report of Wards, Ordinations, Instructions, and General Proceedings of the Bishops and Lesser Priesthood," Church Archives.

"And there is no record of other Church leaders in President Young's lifetime using the 1851 September conference as a text. In short, the Saints seemed to have understood that while "Brother Brigham" had taken a firm stance on obeying the revelation, his celebrated (and often exaggerated) pulpit language—in this case using the threat of excommunication for non-observers—reached beyond his actual policy."

Thomas G. Alexander, in *Mormonism in Transition,* states:

"Although Brigham Young declared the Word of Wisdom to be a commandment and secured the approval of some of the Saints to that proposition, **he announced no revelation on the subject, and actual observance did not coincide with the public pronouncement. An 1851 conference and in some cases other conference addresses or reminiscences of addresses are often cited as the date the Word of Wisdom became binding as a commandment.**

"However, during Brigham Young's lifetime, after the conference, he and other Church leaders and members failed to observe the Word of Wisdom as we interpret it today.

"Brigham Young and other Church leaders again reemphasized the Word of Wisdom in the late 1860s and early 1870s, but this reemphasis seems to have been more closely related to the larger effort to discourage imports than to emphasize the health aspects of the principle.

"From the death of Brigham Young until after the turn of the century, adherence was intermittent. In 1883 and 1884 the general authorities, following the lead of President John Taylor, emphasized the need to adhere to the Word of Wisdom. Thereafter, it seems generally to have laid dormant."

> 4. Peterson, "Word of Wisdom", 55–79; Robert J. McCue, "Did the Word of Wisdom Become a Commandment in 1851?" 66–77; Leonard J. Arrington, "An Economic Interpretation of the Word of Wisdom," 47. **Some of those making statements remembering Brigham Young's declaration that the Word of Wisdom was a commandment included John Taylor in 1853 and Joseph F. Smith in 1909. It seems quite clear, however, that the principle was not generally regarded in the same way as it is today—that is, as essential for holding responsible positions in the Church or for participating in temple ordinances.**

Author's Observations on the 1851 Covenant:

1. By his own public record, Brigham Young did not keep this covenant until 1860 and acknowledged in 1869 that the Word of Wisdom was not a commandment. (See those years)
2. Placing the leaders of the Church under covenant might have been more appropriate given the Prophet Joseph's 1834 decision. Leaders could then have set an example for members.
3. The covenant included "leav(ing) off … all things mentioned in the Word of Wisdom." If this is when the Word of Wisdom became a commandment, then we are now also under commandment to eat meat sparingly.

4. If Brigham Young did excommunicate violators of the Word of Wisdom, that practice soon stopped since senior leaders continued to violate it up until 1921. If leaders had been put under covenant, they could have simply been released for non-observance. Who was to excommunicate Brigham Young, or release him for non-observance?

5. Members are not excommunicated for violating the Word of Wisdom today, but they are typically released from leadership positions and do not receive Temple Recommends, which is more consistent with the Prophet Joseph's standard.

1859 – Brigham Young invokes the name of the Lord against those members drinking liquor:

In 1859 Brigham Young also called upon the men by invoking the name and authority of the Lord to cease their drunkenness, but again he did not say that the Word of Wisdom was now a commandment that the Church should observe to keep.

> **"it is my positive counsel and command that drinking liquor be stopped…In the name of the Lord Jesus Christ, I command the Elders of Israel-those who have been in the habit of getting drunk to cease drinking strong drink from this time henceforth, <u>until you really need it</u>**…As I have already requested, I now again request the authorities of this Church in their various localities to sever from this society those who will not cease getting drunk." (JD 7:338).[10]
>> http://en.wikisource.org/wiki/Journal_of_Discourses/Volume_7/Re-organization_of_the_High_Council%2C_etc.

<u>Author's Comment:</u>

In the days of Joseph Smith and Brigham Young, the proscribed items of the Word of Wisdom were also considered to have medicinal uses, particularly tea and alcohol. Leaders and members alike felt it alright to use these substances during time of illness or "need." For example, during the building up of Nauvoo, the members were plagued with malaria. Joseph is reported to have told members to "make tea and drink it" when river water was unsuitable. He "often made tea and administered it with his own hands." He is also recorded to have drunk wine and beer on occasion."

> See *Saints, Vol 1., 1815-1846, The Standard of Truth*, Chapter 15, note 27. http://www.josephsmithpapers.org/paper-summary/revelation-27-february-1833-dc-89/1#historical-intro

1860 – Brigham Young counsels on chewing tobacco and does not charge those using it with sin:

> "In 1860 he (Brigham Young) said, "Many of the brethren chew tobacco, and I have advised them to be modest about it…Do not glory in this disgraceful practice. If you must use tobacco, **put a small portion in your mouth when no person sees you, and be careful that no one sees you chew it. <u>I do not charge you with sin</u>**. You have the 'Word of Wisdom.' Read it…It is, at least, disgraceful to you to expose your absurdities." (JD 8:362)
>> http://en.wikisource.org/w/index.php?title=Journal_of_Disc ourses/Volume_8/Confession_of_Faults%2C_%26c.&oldid =625921). http://www.somemormonstuff.com/the-word-of-wisdom/

Author's Comment:
1. How could this statement be made if Brigham Young or the Lord declared the Word of Wisdom a commandment in 1851?
2. The statement above is like concerns over the "appearance of evil" that judges those using electronic cigarettes, but unlike Brigham Young, many of today's observers do consider electronic cigarettes to be sin because of the pre-December-2020 Handbook's open-ended proscriptions.

1860 – July: Brigham Young becomes obedient to the Word of Wisdom:

From Paul H. Peterson and Ronald W. Walker, "Brigham Young's Word of Wisdom Legacy," BYU Studies, vol. 42, nos. 3–4 (2003), 29–64:

> "By July 1860, except for medicinal or sacramental reasons, President Young broke off all personal use of alcohol, tobacco, tea, or coffee. Several months later, he spoke of his feat to the Saints, giving as his reason the desire to set a blameless example."I would chew a little in wisdom & would drink a little," he said, "but I will not do it to have our little children chew [that are] a few years old.""[102]
>> 102 Brigham Young, Sermon, General Church Minutes, October 28, 1860

1861 – June: Brigham Young reports he has given up chewing tobacco:

From Paul H. Peterson and Ronald W. Walker, "Brigham Young's Word of Wisdom Legacy," BYU Studies, vol. 42, nos. 3–4 (2003), 29–64:

> "He hoped that the Saints would likewise control themselves. "I have used tobacco a great portion of my life, and I have quit it," he told the Saints in Centerville, Utah, in June 1861. "Some will say to me how in the world could you do it. Because I was a mind to," he said. "Can you do the same? Yes.""[103]
>> 103 Brigham Young, Sermon, General Church Minutes, June 30, 1861.

1862 – October: Brigham Young reports he became Word of Wisdom observant in 1860:

From Paul H. Peterson and Ronald W. Walker, "Brigham Young's Word of Wisdom Legacy," BYU Studies, vol. 42, nos. 3–4 (2003), 29–64:

> "He gave similar advice at October general conference in 1862. "I have been in the habit of using tobacco a great deal in my life, but it is now almost two years and a half since I have tasted it,""

1865 – Brigham Young on Tobacco, Tea, and Coffee:

> "Brigham Young's policy was to walk a fine line between preaching adherence and leaving people free to choose. In 1865 he preached, "Let us raise our own tobacco, or quit using it…**The Lord gave me strength to lay aside tobacco, and it is very rarely indeed that I taste tea or coffee; yet I have no objection to aged persons, when they are fatigued and feel infirm, taking a little stimulus that will do them good.""** (JD 11:140-141
>> http://en.wikisource.org/wiki/Journal_of_Discourses/Volume_11/Home_Manufacturing%2C_Merchandising%2C_and_General_Economy).
>> http://www.somemormonstuff.com/the-word-of-wisdom/

1868 – April: Brigham Young preaches against meat:

From Paul H. Peterson and Ronald W. Walker, "Brigham Young's
Word of Wisdom Legacy," BYU Studies, vol. 42, nos. 3–4 (2003),
29–64, Note 118:

> "118 Brigham Young, Remarks, "Minutes of the Provo
> School of the Prophets," April 15, 1868.
> In February 1860, Brigham Young admitted to a close group
> of confidantes, that he found Hyrum Smith's position on the
> Word of Wisdom incongruous. "Hyrum would eat about three
> lb of fat pork in a day," Brigham noted incredulously, "and yet
> be so severe upon a tobacco chewer." Brigham Young
> Office Journal, February 24, 1860, Book D, August 8, 1858
> to September 30, 1863. In April conference 1868, both
> President Young and Apostle George Q. Cannon railed
> against pork eating. Elder Cannon said that "swine's flesh
> should be entirely abstained from," while Brigham Young,
> presumably speaking after Cannon, noted that "it was the
> will of the Lord that his people should cease eating swine's
> flesh." "History of the Church," April 6, 1868, 1839–[ca.
> 1882], Historian's Office, Church Archives. At an April 1868
> School of the Prophets meeting in Provo, Brigham Young
> told assembled members that swine flesh was unhealthy.
> Two weeks later, speaking again with school members,
> Brigham advised everyone "to refrain from eating such
> meat."
>> Young, Remarks, "Minutes of the Provo School of the
>> Prophets," April 15, 27, 1868."

**1869 – 7 April: Brigham Young acknowledges the Word of
Wisdom is not a commandment except under the Oath and
Covenant of the Priesthood which he appears to apply to all
members:**

> **"I know that some say the revelations upon these (Word
> of Wisdom) points are not given by way of
> commandment. <u>Very well</u>, but we are commanded to
> observe every word that proceeds from the mouth of
> God."**
>> Young, Brigham. *Discourses of Brigham Young.* Selected
>> by John A. Widtsoe. 1941. pgs, 182-33

<u>**Author's Comment:**</u>
President Young was speaking in the new Tabernacle. He is generally encouraging all members to keep the Word of Wisdom, but in this argument, he uses a scripture that is limited to those who have taken upon them the Oath and Covenant of the Priesthood (D&C 84: 43-44) and acknowledges ("Very well") that the Word of Wisdom was not given as a commandment.

1870 – October: Brigham Young on Word of Wisdom interpretation and obedience:

> **That it was "not by commandment" is affirmed by Brigham Young in a sermon given October 30, 1870:** "In some respects we have to define it for ourselves—each for himself—according to our own views, judgment and faith, and the observance of the Word of Wisdom…must be left, partially, with the people…We cannot say you shall never drink a cup of tea, or you shall never taste of this, or you shall never taste of that; but we can say that Wisdom is justified of her children"
>> (JD 14:20.
>> http://en.wikisource.org/wiki/Journal_of_Discourses/Volum e_14/The_Fashions_of_the_World%2C_etc.)
>> http://www.somemormonstuff.com/the-word-of-wisdom/

1877 – April: Brigham Young requires Word of Wisdom obedience for entering the Saint George Temple – the first Temple in the West:

From Paul H. Peterson and Ronald W. Walker, "Brigham Young's Word of Wisdom Legacy," BYU Studies, vol. 42, nos. 3–4 (2003), 29–64:
> "When he drew up a list of worthiness criteria to gauge the spiritual level of individual Saints in the St. George Stake, the Word of Wisdom appeared first. Perhaps intended as a guideline for admission to the recently completed temple, the worthiness list was similar to the catechism used in the 1856–1857 Reformation, but now the question posed for Word of Wisdom obedience no longer concerned just "drunkenness." **Religiously active Church members "must observe and keep the Word of Wisdom according to the Spirit and meaning thereof," it said."** [137]
>> 137 Brigham Young to J. D. T. McAllister, April 13, 1877, Brigham Young Letterbooks.

1877 – May: Brigham Young requires missionaries not living the Word of Wisdom to be sent home:

From Paul H. Peterson and Ronald W. Walker, "Brigham Young's Word of Wisdom Legacy," BYU Studies, vol. 42, nos. 3–4 (2003), 29–64:

> "And in May 1877, only months before his death, President Young included strong Word of Wisdom counsel in instructions given to Elder Joseph F. Smith, recently called to preside over the European Mission: missionaries who could not abstain from tobacco and alcohol were to be sent home." [138]
>
>> 138 Brigham Young to Joseph F. Smith, May 11, 1877, Brigham Young Letterbooks

1898 – President Wilford Woodruff declines to make the Word of Wisdom a Temple Recommend Requirement and that members should be "taught to refrain from meat":
In 1898 it is still evident from a meeting of the First Presidency and the Twelve, that the Lord had not given any further instruction on the Word of Wisdom and **President Woodruff "did not think that Bishops should withhold recommends from persons who did not adhere strictly to it."**

> "THE STATUS OF THE WORD OF WISDOM at the turn of the century is evident from contemporary sources. At a meeting on May 5,1898, the First Presidency and Twelve discussed the Word of Wisdom. One member read from the twelfth volume of the Journal of Discourses a statement by Brigham Young that seemed to support the notion that the Word of Wisdom was a commandment of God. Lorenzo Snow, then President of the Council of the Twelve agreed, saying that he believed the Word of Wisdom was a commandment and that it should be carried out to the letter. In doing so, he said, members should be taught to refrain from eating meat except in dire necessity, because Joseph Smith had taught that animals have spirits. **Wilford Woodruff, then President of the Church, said he looked upon the Word of Wisdom as a commandment and that all members should observe it, but for the present, no definite action should be taken except that the members should be taught to refrain from meat.**

"The minutes of the meeting record that **"President Woodruff said he regarded the Word of Wisdom in its entirety as given of the Lord for the Latter-day Saints to observe, but he did not think that Bishops should withhold recommends from persons who did not adhere strictly to it.""**1

1 Diary of Heber J. Grant, May 5, and June 30, 1898, LDS Church Archives; "Journal History of the Church of Jesus Christ of Latter-day Saints" (JH), May 5, 1898, LDS Church Archives, Microcopy in BYU Library. See George D. Watt, etal. eds Journal of Discourses, 26 Vols. (Liverpool, 1855-85), 12: 27ff

Taken from THE WORD OF WISDOM: FROM PRINCIPLE TO REQUIREMENT by THOMAS G. ALEXANDER

1902 – President Joseph F. Smith urges withholding recommends from "flagrant (Word of Wisdom) violators":

Thomas G. Alexander, in *Mormonism in Transition,* states:

"The death of Lorenzo Snow brought to the presidency Joseph F. Smith, who held views on the Word of Wisdom very close to those of Elder Grant. **The path to the current interpretation of the Word of Wisdom leads from Smith's administration. Dropping the emphasis on abstaining from meat, he urged the need to refrain from the use of tea, coffee, alcohol, and tobacco.** In 1902 he reversed President Snow's tolerant ruling and closed the saloon at Saltair, a move that the Protestant clergy heartily approved. Apparently following this lead, in June 1902 the First Presidency and Twelve agreed not to fellowship anyone who operated or frequented saloons. In the same year Joseph F. Smith urged stake presidents and others to refuse recommends to flagrant violators, but to be somewhat liberal with old men who used tobacco and old ladies who drank tea. He said, however, that Bishops should deny temple recommends to habitual drunkards." 9

9. Thomas Hull, "Events of the Month," 559, and "Saltair and Temperance," 731; Lund, Journal, June 26, 1902; First Presidency, Letter to C. R. Hakes, August 1, 1902, First Presidency Letters; First Presidency, Letter to John W. Hess, October 31, 1902, First Presidency Letters; First Presidency, Letter to H. S. Allen, November 1, 1902, First Presidency Letters.

<u>**Author's Comment:**</u>
Why drop the Lord's emphasis on meat? How many lives of Latter-day Saints could have been extended with useful service in building up the Kingdom of God, if they had not been burdened with the multiple Western diseases that spring from excessive meat consumption.

1913 – President Joseph F. Smith on why the Word of Wisdom was not given as a Commandment:

> "The reason undoubtedly why the Word of Wisdom was given—as not by 'commandment or restraint' was that at that time, at least, if it had been given as a commandment it would have brought every man, addicted to the use of these noxious things, under condemnation; so the Lord was merciful and gave them a chance to overcome, before He brought them under the law." [16]
>> President Joseph F. Smith, *Conference Report* (October 1913), 14.

<u>**Author's Comment:**</u>
Two questions arise from this statement:
1. When did the Lord bring "them under the law"? No revelation is cited including the Oath and Covenant of the Priesthood; however, the Prophet Joseph did bring leaders under the law in 1834 and many early members were reported following the Word of Wisdom exactly!
2. What of new members who entered the Church with addictions; would not "the Lord (be) merciful and g(i)ve them a chance to overcome, before He brought them under the law"?

1915 – President Joseph F. Smith restricts tobacco and "intoxicating drinks":
President Joseph F. Smith does not cite the Lord declaring the Word of Wisdom a commandment, but by 1915 the standard is beginning to be enforced with respect to tobacco and "intoxicating drinks."

Taken from THE WORD OF WISDOM: FROM PRINCIPLE TO REQUIREMENT by THOMAS G. ALEXANDER:

> "… In the meantime, emphasis on the Word of Wisdom during Joseph F. Smith's administration continued essentially as in 1902.
>
> "In a letter dated December 28, 1915, **President Smith said that young "or middle-aged men who have had experience in the Church should not be ordained to the Priesthood nor recommended to the privileges of the House of the Lord unless they will abstain from the use of tobacco and intoxicating drinks.""**14
>> Joseph F. Smith to C. Elmo Cluff, December 28, 1915, Joseph F. Smith Letterbooks, Church Archives; Improvement Era, March 16, 1916, p. 461; ibid., April, 1917, pp. 555-58; ibid., November, 1917, pp. 11, 64; ibid., March 1919, pp. 371-80; Relief Society Magazine, February, 1918, p.160; April, 1919, pp. 238-39; February, 1918, p. 146; September, 1919, pp. 527, 593.

1917 – The question of Caffeine:
Issues on Caffeine products is an example of no additional direct revelation on the Word of Wisdom.

> "… In addition to liquor, tobacco, tea and coffee, some members of the Church urged that the prohibitions of the Word of Wisdom ought to be broader. In March 1917, Frederick J. Pack of the University of Utah published an article in the Improvement Era dealing with the question, "Should LDS Drink CocaCola?" His answer was no. His argument was not that the Word of Wisdom prohibited such drinks, but that such drinks contained the same drugs as tea and coffee." 25
>> 25 Improvement Era, March 1971, pp. 432-35.

"… while the First Presidency has taken no official stand on the use of cola drinks, some members urge abstinence."26

> 26 Grant Diary, October 15, November 11, 12, and 16, 1924; First Presidency Letter of May 6, 1971, Edgemont South Stake Letter Files. See also Lester E. Bush, Jr., ed. "Mormon Medical Ethical Guidelines," Dialogue: A Journal of Mormon Thought XII (No. 3), pp. 102-104, for the only official guidance to date on cola drinks
> Taken from THE WORD OF WISDOM: FROM PRINCIPLE TO REQUIREMENT by THOMAS G. ALEXANDER

<u>Author's Comment:</u>

The 2010 through pre-Dec-2020-Handbook proscribed Caffeine since it was "habit-forming" but was not enforced.

38.7.13   Word of Wisdom

"… Nor should members use harmful or habit-forming substances except under the care of a competent physician."

<u>**IMPOSITION**</u> rather than "greeting … revelation and … wisdom":
1921-PRESENT

1921 – President Heber J. Grant establishes today's Standard for Obedience to the Word of Wisdom for a Temple Recommend:
It is President Grant in 1921 who established the standard enforced today.

> <u>In 1921, the Lord inspired President Heber J. Grant to call on all Saints to live the Word of Wisdom to the letter by completely abstaining from all alcohol, coffee, tea, and tobacco.</u> Today Church members are expected to live this higher standard.17
>
>> 17 Moderation rather than abstinence was applied to virtually all of the "do nots" of the Word of Wisdom until the early 20th century. On the tightening up of Word of Wisdom observance, see Thomas G. Alexander, Mormonism in Transition: A History of the Latter-day Saints, 1890–1930 (Urbana: University of Illinois Press, 1986), 258–71; Paul H. Peterson and Ronald W. Walker, "Brigham Young's Word of Wisdom Legacy," BYU Studies, vol. 42, nos. 3–4 (2003), 29–64. https://history.lds.org/article/doctrine-and-covenants-word-of-wisdom?lang=eng

> After the inauguration of Heber J. Grant's administration in 1918, however, the advice became less flexible. <u>In 1921, church leadership made adherence to the Word of Wisdom a requirement for admission to the temple.</u> Before this stake presidents and bishops had been encouraged to in this matter, but exceptions had been made. Apparently under this new emphasis, in March, 1921, George F. Richards, both as apostle and president of the Salt Lake Temple, phoned two Salt Lake City bishops about two tobacco users who had come to the temple and told the bishops "to try to clean them up before they come here again."15
>
>> 15 George F. Richards Journal, March 26, 1921. Information on the Temple recommend bookfrom K. Heybron Adams, formerly of the LDS Church Archives. Thomas G. Alexander, Mormonism in Transition: A History of the Latter-day Saints, 1890–1930

<u>**Author's Comment:**</u>
1. The Spirit witnesses to me that President Heber J. Grant was correct in understanding the Lord's will that the Word of Wisdom (D&C 89) be followed by those entering upon Temple Covenants. Such individuals are under the Oath and Covenant of the Priesthood's commandment to "live by every word that proceedeth forth from the mouth of God." (D&C 84: 43-44) Rather than being a new policy, this action serves to restore Joseph Smith's requirement that all leaders be obedient to the Word of Wisdom.
2. I found no record of this decision or letter. Is there any revelation cited? Does it apply strictly to those seeking a Temple Recommend or to "all saints" as the Church website suggests?

1930 – President Grant restricts missionaries:

"… Heber J. Grant in January 1930 warned bishops that young men using tobacco were not to be called on missions."
> Taken from THE WORD OF WISDOM: FROM PRINCIPLE TO REQUIREMENT by THOMAS G. ALEXANDER

<u>**Author's Comment:**</u>
1. Since missionaries prior to 1930 were not required to live the Word of Wisdom, it is reasonable to assert that obedience to the Word of Wisdom was not required for converts. That may have changed when President Grant made this change in the requirements for serving as a missionary. Certainly by 1955, when my father was baptized, he was required to stop smoking and the use of alcohol. During my mission to the Philippines (1968-1970) Word of Wisdom obedience was required for baptism.
2. Records for this period appear very scant or were not made available to historians whose works I accessed. I have not located any letters detailing these changes in Word of Wisdom policy.

1933 – General Handbook changes:

"Between 1921 and 1933, the adherence to the Word of Wisdom for full fellowship in the Church was made even more explicit. The 1928 General Handbook of Instructions, to guide bishops and stake presidents on church policy, reads: "It is important that all those who may desire to enter the temple for endowments or other ordinances should be encouraged by the bishopric to observe the principle of tithing as well as all other Gospel principles.

"The next edition of the Handbook, published in 1933, reads that members desiring temple recommends "should observe the law of tithing. The applicant should also observe all other principles of the Gospel, should keep the Word of Wisdom, not use profanity, should not join nor be a member of any secret oath bound organization and should sustain without reservation the general and local authorities of the church." Additionally, both the 1928 and 1934 editions of the Handbook — but not previous editions—listed "liquor drinking" and "bootlegging" among the "transgressions which are ordinarily such as to justify consideration by the bishop's court." To these the 1934 edition also added "drunkenness.""16

> 16 LDS Church, Handbook of Instructions, No. 14, 1928 (n.p., 1928), p. 11; idem. Handbook of Instructions, No. 15, 1934 (n.p., 1933), p. 10.
> Taken from **THE WORD OF WISDOM: FROM PRINCIPLE TO REQUIREMENT**, THOMAS G. ALEXANDER (https://www.dialoguejournal.com/wp-content/uploads/sbi/articles/Dialogue_V14N03_80.pdf)

2010 – General Handbook 2 adds sweeping proscriptions. The role of Revelation reviewed:

Handbook 2 clarifies "hot drinks", includes illegal drugs which clearly is sin by violation of the law of the land, and adds sweeping additional proscriptions against "harmful or habit-forming substances."

21.3.11   Word of Wisdom

"The only official interpretation of "hot drinks" (D&C 89:9) in the Word of Wisdom is the statement made by early Church leaders that the term "hot drinks" means tea and coffee.

"Members should not use any substance that contains illegal drugs. Nor should members use harmful or habit-forming substances except under the care of a competent physician."

Electronic cigarettes and legal marijuana come under the broad category of "habit-forming substances." No new revelation from the Lord is cited to support this broad expansion of Word of Wisdom proscriptions. Enforcement for obtaining baptism or Temple Recommends is unclear, since the question posed to the candidate is simply "Do you keep the Word of Wisdom?" Judgement is left to the individual except where Mission Presidents, Bishops or Stake Presidents enforce interpretations based on Handbook 2.

What role revelation has played throughout this history of Word of Wisdom application is addressed by Roy W. Doxey, and Thomas G. Alexander. The prophets have also addressed it in that there has been no claim to new direct revelation from the Lord. Prayerful debate has been the norm with outside influences such as Utah politics and US national movements against alcohol and Tobacco playing a role.

"... What role did revelation play in the matter? It is clear that Section 89 of the Doctrine and Covenants was given as a revelation to Joseph Smith. Advice that the members of the Church adhere to the Word of Wisdom was also undoubtedly given under inspiration. **There is, however, no known contemporary evidence of which I am aware that a separate new revelation changed the Word of Wisdom from a "principle with promise" to "a commandment" necessary for full participation in all the blessings of church membership.**

"One author on the subject has argued that the vote in 1880 sustaining the Doctrine and Covenants as binding on church membership was equivalent to a vote making the Word of Wisdom a commandment. If, however, the members were voting on the words contained in the book, what they did was to agree that the Word of Wisdom was "a principle with promise" not a commandment." 28

28 Roy W. Doxey, The Word of Wisdom Today (Salt Lake City: Deseret Book Company, 1975), pp. 13-14.

"… It is much easier, therefore, to find references to previous statements than to see the presence of new, specific revelation. The inclusion of coffee and tea and the exclusion of cocoa, for instance, from the prohibited substances can probably be attributed to statements of Joseph and Hyrum Smith and Brigham Young rather than to specific revelations."29

29 Some of the statements and reminiscences are cited in Doxey, pp. 10-13 and in John A. Widtsoe and Leah D. Widtsoe, The Word of Wisdom: A Modern Interpretation (Salt Lake City: Deseret Book Company, 1937), p. 28. **Here I am speaking of specific revelations rather than the type of revelation mentioned later in this article. I would differentiate between what might be termed instant and unexpected revelations and revelations derived from long and prayerful consideration of a particular problem under the inspiration of the Holy Spirit.** Taken from THE WORD OF WISDOM: FROM PRINCIPLE TO REQUIREMENT, THOMAS G. ALEXANDER (https://www.dialoguejournal.com/wp-content/uploads/sbi/articles/Dialogue_V14N03_80.pdf)

2019 – Vaping, green tea and coffee-based products prohibited.
On 15 August 2019, an Official Church Statement on the Word of
Wisdom, added more "prohibited" items:

> "The Word of Wisdom is a law of health for the physical and
> spiritual benefit of God's children. It includes instruction
> about what foods are good for us and those substances to
> avoid. Over time, Church leaders have provided additional
> instruction on those things that are encouraged or forbidden
> by the Word of Wisdom, and have taught that substances
> that are destructive, habit-forming or addictive should be
> avoided.
>
> "In recent publications for Church members, Church leaders
> have clarified that several substances are prohibited by the
> Word of Wisdom, including vaping or e-cigarettes, green tea,
> and coffee-based products. They also have cautioned that
> substances such as marijuana and opioids should be used
> only for medicinal purposes as prescribed by a competent
> physician."
>> https://newsroom.churchofjesuschrist.org/article/statement
>> -word-of-wisdom-august-2019

2020 – The December 2020 Handbook significantly changed Word of Wisdom policy by removing all 2010 proscriptions on "members use (of) harmful or habit-forming substances except under the care of a competent physician" except for marijuana. However, the Church retained the view that "The Word of Wisdom is a commandment of God."

The Handbook now states:

38.7.13.

"The Word of Wisdom is a commandment of God. He revealed it for the physical and spiritual benefit of His children. Prophets have clarified that the teachings in Doctrine and Covenants 89 include **abstinence** from tobacco, strong drinks (alcohol), and hot drinks (tea and coffee).

"Prophets have also taught members to **avoid** substances that are harmful, illegal, or addictive or that impair judgment.

"There are other harmful substances and practices that are not specified in the Word of Wisdom or by Church leaders. Members should **use wisdom and prayerful judgment in making choices** to promote their physical, spiritual, and emotional health.

"The Apostle Paul stated: "Know ye not that your body is the temple of the Holy Ghost which is in you, which ye have of God, and ye are not your own? For ye are bought with a price: therefore glorify God in your body, and in your spirit, which are God's" (1 Corinthians 6:19–20).

"The Lord promises spiritual and temporal blessings to those who obey the Word of Wisdom and the guidance of living prophets (see Doctrine and Covenants 89:18–21)."

… and for Medical Marijuana:

38.7.9

"The Church opposes the use of marijuana for non-medical purposes. See "Word of Wisdom and Healthy Practices" (38.7.13).

"However, marijuana may be used for medicinal purposes when the following conditions are met:

> "The use is determined to be medically necessary by a licensed physician or another legally approved medical provider.

> "The person follows the dosage and mode of administration from the physician or other authorized medical provider. The Church does not approve of vaping marijuana unless the medical provider has authorized it based on medical necessity.

"The Church does not approve of smoking marijuana, including for medical purposes."

Author's Comment:
President Russell M. Nelson's update to the Word of Wisdom in December 2020 removes the additional restrictions that can only be used "under the care of a competent physician" completely, except for marijuana under medical permission.

The clear implication is that the stunning list of additional prohibitions that have burdened Church members and restrained investigators since at least 2010, had not been received by revelation, but because of the best intentions of Church leaders.

Also, this new policy on the Word of Wisdom replaces the 15 August 2019 Official Church Statement by its currency – previous policy statements are consolidated or removed by the Handbook update. Hence the vaping, green tea, and coffee products policy is gone – "hot drinks" as stated by the Lord and defined by the Prophet Joseph Smith as hot tea (which is green tea) and coffee is restored.

The Lord's "not(s)" are restored. All that we need now is for the leaders of the Church to gain an understanding of the Lord's phrase describing the Word of Wisdom as given "not by commandment or constraint, but … showing forth the <u>order</u> and will of God" as was correctly applied by the Prophet Joseph Smith and described in this work.

I have every confidence in what the Lord taught me within my stewardship about the Word of Wisdom. That knowledge, along with this December 2020 partial restoration, gives me every confidence that the truth about the Word of Wisdom will once again be fully restored and understood to the benefit of God's children and their greater access to the grace of His Son.

www.ingramcontent.com/pod-product-compliance
Lightning Source LLC
Chambersburg PA
CBHW071444130726
47997CB00006B/2227